MODERN APPLICATIONS WITH PYTHON

Web Development with Flask and FastAPI

Diego Rodrigues

MASTERTECH
MODERN APPLICATIONS
WITH PYTHON
Web Development with Flask and FastAPI

2025 Edition
Author: Diego Rodrigues

Published by StudioD21.

Important Note

The codes and scripts presented in this book aim to illustrate the concepts discussed in the chapters, serving as practical examples. These examples were developed in custom, controlled environments, and therefore there is no guarantee that they will work fully in all scenarios. It is essential to check the configurations and customizations of the environment where they will be applied to ensure their proper functioning. We thank you for your understanding.

CONTENTS

GREETINGS!

Hello, dear reader!

It is a great pleasure to welcome you on this journey through the universe of modern web development with **Python, Flask e FastAPI**. Your decision to explore and master these technologies demonstrates an innovative mindset and continuous search for strategic technical knowledge. This book, **"MODERN APPLICATIONS WITH PYTHON: Web Development with Flask and FastAPI"**, has been carefully designed to be the most complete and practical guide available on the subject, empowering you to create robust, scalable, and efficient APIs and applications.

We live in an era where the web is the heart of digital transformation, connecting companies, people and systems in increasingly sophisticated ways. Frameworks such as Flask and FastAPI represent the most modern and efficient development of web applications and APIs, allowing the creation of agile and performant solutions. Professionals and companies that master these tools have an immense competitive advantage in the market. This book was structured exactly to provide this knowledge, ensuring that you can learn, apply and evolve in web development with Python in a clear and objective way.

Throughout this reading, you will go through a progressive evolution, from the **web development fundamentals** until the creation of **Advanced APIs and scalable applications**. We will explore everything from essential concepts, such as HTTP, REST and web architecture, to modern practices such as **static typing, authentication, database integration, security**

and efficient deployment. All this accompanied by practical examples, step-by-step guides and strategic tips so that you can implement this knowledge in your daily life.

This book was prepared with a didactic and pragmatic commitment, following the guidelines of **Protocolo TECHWRITE 2.0**, ensuring that the learning experience is fluid, dynamic and immediately applicable. The content was developed so that you can **read and code at the same time**, allowing each concept learned to be put into practice instantly.

Whether you're a beginning developer, a seasoned professional looking to refresh your knowledge, or someone who wants to create powerful web applications from scratch, this book will be your definitive guide to mastering Flask and FastAPI.

Get ready to transform your knowledge and elevate your web development skills with Python!

Happy reading and much success!

ABOUT THE AUTHOR

www.linkedin.com/in/diegoexpertai

Best-Selling Author, Diego Rodrigues is an International Consultant and Writer specializing in Market Intelligence, Technology and Innovation. With 42 international certifications from institutions such as IBM, Google, Microsoft, AWS, Cisco, and Boston University, Ec-Council, Palo Alto and META.

Rodrigues is an expert in Artificial Intelligence, Machine Learning, Data Science, Big Data, Blockchain, Connectivity Technologies, Ethical Hacking and Threat Intelligence.

Since 2003, Rodrigues has developed more than 200 projects for important brands in Brazil, USA and Mexico. In 2024, he consolidates himself as one of the largest new generation authors of technical books in the world, with more than 180 titles published in six languages.

PRESENTATION OF THE BOOK

Web development with **Python** has evolved significantly in recent years, becoming one of the pillars of modern technology. Frameworks like **Flask e FastAPI** play a crucial role in creating **Efficient, scalable and high-performance APIs**, enabling companies and developers to build robust applications quickly and flexibly. Mastering these technologies is no longer an option, but an essential requirement for anyone who wants to stand out in the web development and API-first market.

This book has been carefully crafted to be the **most complete and practical guide** about Flask and FastAPI available today, covering everything from fundamental concepts to advanced applications and professional deployment strategies. Our mission is to provide a material **affordable, up-to-date and highly applicable**, which allows you to not only understand technologies, but also implement them efficiently in real-world projects.

The structure of the book was designed to provide a **fluid and progressive experience**, combining **theory and practice** in a balanced way. No **Chapter 1**, we begin with an overview of the **web development with Python**, exploring its growth, its importance in the current ecosystem and the advantages of the chosen frameworks. Then, in **Chapter 2**, we approach **development environment configuration**, ensuring you have all the tools you need to start coding productively.

No **Chapter 3**, we review you **essential fundamentals of Python for the web,** including data structures, file manipulation and modularization, ensuring that even those with little experience can follow the content. Already in **Chapter 4**, we explore the **principles of HTTP and RESTful APIs**, fundamental elements for any modern web application.

From the **Chapter 5**, we dive into **Flask**, starting with its basic concepts, advantages and initial structure. Node **Chapter 6**, we detail the **routing and organization of routes**, essential for building well-structured APIs. Node **Chapter 7**, we present the **templating system with Jinja2**, allowing you to create dynamic and reusable pages.

Form manipulation and data validation are covered in **Chapter 8**, while the **Chapter 9** focus on **integration with databases using SQLAlchemy and ORM**, covering data modeling and CRUD operations. Node **Chapter 10**, we deal with **authentication and authorization**, ensuring that your application is secure and reliable.

We know that **errors and debugging** are an inevitable part of the development process, so the **Chapter 11** addresses strategies for **troubleshooting no Flask**, helping to solve common problems.

The second part of the book focuses on **FastAPI**, starting at **Chapter 12**, where we explain the concepts and advantages of this ultra-fast framework. Node **Chapter 13**, we created the first APIs using FastAPI, while in **Chapter 14**, we explore **static typing and data validation with Pydantic**, one of the tool's biggest differentiators.

A **automatic documentation** generated by FastAPI is the theme of **Chapter 15**, where we show how to use Swagger and Redoc to create well-documented APIs. Node **Chapter 16**, we approach **integration with databases**, using SQLAlchemy and advanced techniques for data manipulation.

Security is a critical aspect of any API, and in **Chapter 17**, we discussed the **implementing authentication and access control with JWT and OAuth2**. No **Chapter 18**, we focus on

deployment and scalability, teaching how to prepare your application to run on ASGI servers, with optimization for high performance.

No **Chapter 19**, we explore **automated testing and code quality best practices**, fundamental to maintaining reliable software. Already in **Chapter 20**, we present guidelines for **code standardization and organization**, ensuring long-term maintainability.

THE **Chapter 21** copper **debugging and monitoring**, teaching how to diagnose and solve problems proactively. Node **Chapter 22**, we discussed **microservices and distributed architectures**, an essential paradigm for scalable systems.

For a more comprehensive understanding, the **Chapter 23** it presents **modern web development architectures**, exploring patterns such as MVC and MVVM. Node **Chapter 24**, we show **how to integrate frontends and consume APIs**, ensuring a fluid experience between the backend and the user interface.

Real use cases are analyzed in the **Chapter 25**, where we study successful applications and learn from challenges faced in the market. Performance optimization, essential for scalable applications, is the focus of **Chapter 26**, with advanced techniques to improve response time and resource consumption.

THE **Chapter 27** addresses the **dependency management and virtual environments**, featuring tools like pipenv and poetry for an efficient development flow. Node **Chapter 28**, we explore **complementary tools and libraries**, expanding your possibilities with powerful extensions.

THE **Chapter 29** provides insight into **trends and innovations in web development with Python**, analyzing new emerging technologies and the impact of AI on the sector. Finally, in the **Chapter 30**, we discussed **strategies for maintaining and evolving web projects**, ensuring that your applications remain efficient and relevant over time.

This book has been structured to ensure that you not only understand the essential concepts of Flask and FastAPI, but are also able to apply them practically and strategically. If you want **create powerful APIs, develop modern web applications, and become an expert in the Python ecosystem**, this reading will be a turning point in your journey.

Now it's time to dive into the world of modern web development with **Flask e FastAPI**. Let's explore best practices together and build incredible applications!

CHAPTER 1. INTRODUCTION TO WEB DEVELOPMENT WITH PYTHON

Web development has undergone a remarkable transformation over the past few decades. At the beginning of the internet, pages were built statically, with basic HTML and simple visual elements. Over time, the need for interactivity and dynamism drove the evolution of the technologies involved. Languages like JavaScript began to play an essential role in creating richer experiences, while frameworks and libraries made development work easier.

The advent of the client-server model brought the need for languages that were capable of managing **HTTP requests, manipulate databases and process business logic efficiently**. Python has emerged as one of the leading languages for this purpose due to its **simplicity, readability and abstraction power**.

Frameworks for web development began to gain ground, offering structured and efficient solutions for creating scalable applications. Initially, tools like CGI and mod_python were explored, but they quickly gave way to more modern solutions like **Django, Flask and more recently FastAPI**, each serving different needs in the web development ecosystem.

Python's Role in Digital Transformation

Python has established itself as one of the most influential and widely used languages in the world of technology, impacting not only web development, but several areas, such as **data science, artificial intelligence, automation and cloud**

computing. Its clear and expressive syntax allows developers to create robust applications with less code and greater readability, making maintenance more efficient.

In the context of web development, **Python** brought a more pragmatic and lean approach. Unlike languages like Java, which have a more rigid and bureaucratic structure, Python allows you to develop quickly **APIs, web services and scalable applications** with flexible and powerful frameworks. This caused companies to adopt the language in their products, boosting its popularity.

Furthermore, **Python** has become the basis of large platforms and services. Companies like **Google, Instagram, Netflix and Spotify** use the language in their ecosystems, which validates their ability to deal with complex applications. Its compatibility with databases, ability to integrate with modern technologies, and support for scalability make it one of the most strategic choices for software developers and architects.

Overview of Flask and FastAPI frameworks

Frameworks play a fundamental role in web development, as they offer organized frameworks, optimized tools and best practices for creating efficient applications. Among the various options available, **Flask** and **FastAPI** stand out as agile and powerful solutions for building APIs and scalable web systems.

Flask: Flexibility and Simplicity

Flask is a **microframework** which offers a minimalist approach to web development. Unlike more robust frameworks like Django, Flask provides **total developer freedom**, allowing the application architecture to be defined according to the project's needs.

Its modular design makes it easy to integrate with external libraries and tools, making it ideal for projects that require customization. Flask allows you to build REST APIs in a practical way, enabling everything from simple applications to complex systems, using extensions that expand their functionalities.

Flask main features:

- Light and flexible structure
- Support for dynamic routing
- Templating system with Jinja2
- Ease of integration with databases via SQLAlchemy
- Middleware support and custom authentication

FastAPI: Performance and Static Typing

FastAPI emerged as a response to the need for ultra-fast and efficient frameworks for API development. Based on ASGI (Asynchronous Server Gateway Interface), it allows the creation of highly performant asynchronous applications, optimizing server resource consumption.

Furthermore, its integration with Pydantic offers native support for static typing and data validation, ensuring security and efficiency in information manipulation. Its OpenAPI compatibility and automatic documentation make FastAPI a robust choice for modern projects.

Main advantages of FastAPI:

- Exceptional performance due to asynchronous execution
- Static typing and automatic validation with Pydantic
- Automatic generation of interactive documentation (Swagger and Redoc)
- Native integration with WebSockets and GraphQL
- Ideal for modern applications and microservices

While Flask offers simplicity and flexibility, FastAPI brings performance and robustness, allowing developers to choose the best approach for each need.

Objectives and structure of the book

The purpose of this material is to provide a complete and highly educational guide on web development with Python, covering everything from fundamental concepts to advanced applications. This book has been structured to ensure progressive learning, combining theory and practice, with direct explanations and applicable codes.

The structure of the book is divided into three main axes:

1. **Fundamentals of web development with Python**: Explanation of essential concepts, protocols, databases and support tools.
2. **Practical applications with Flask and FastAPI**: Building APIs, data manipulation, authentication and security.
3. **Optimization and deployment**: Advanced scalability techniques, continuous integration and modern development practices.

Each chapter contains practical examples and detailed explanations, allowing the reader to learn not only the theory, but how to apply it effectively. The intention is to ensure that at the end of reading, you are able to develop complete, secure and scalable web applications with Python.

From here, we'll explore each aspect of these technologies, demonstrating best practices for developing **Modern, optimized, high-performance APIs.**

CHAPTER 2. CONFIGURING THE DEVELOPMENT ENVIRONMENT

To begin web development with Python, it is essential to ensure that the environment is configured correctly. Python is already installed by default on some Linux distributions and macOS, but the version may be out of date. The ideal is to always have the latest version to take advantage of new features and optimizations.

On Windows, the official installer can be downloaded from the official Python website. During installation, the "Add Python to PATH" option must be checked to allow the use of the interpreter directly in the terminal.

Installation check:

bash

```
python --version
```

If it is necessary to install or update, the command below can be used on Debian-based Linux distributions:

bash

```
sudo apt update && sudo apt install python3
```

On Red Hat-based distributions:

bash

```
sudo dnf install python3
```

For macOS, the Homebrew manager makes installation easy:

bash

```
brew install python
```

Package management is essential for efficient development. THE pip is the default package manager and allows you to install libraries directly from the official Python repository.

bash

```
pip install flask fastapi
```

Other options, such as pipenv and poetry, offer more refined control over dependencies, ensuring isolation and reproducibility of environments.

Configuring virtual environments

Virtual environments avoid conflicts between projects, ensuring that each one uses its own dependencies without interference from global packages. THE venv is the tool integrated into Python that allows you to create and manage these environments.

To create a new virtual environment:

bash

```
python -m venv myenv
```

Environment activation depends on the operating system:

- Windows:

bash

```
myenv\Scripts\activate
```

- Linux/macOS:

bash

```
source myenv/bin/activate
```

The terminal will indicate that the virtual environment is active. In this state, any installed package will be restricted to this environment, avoiding impacts on other projects.

To deactivate:

bash

```
deactivate
```

Tools like pipenv manage dependencies and environments in an integrated way. To start a new project with pipenv:

bash

```
pip install pipenv
pipenv install flask
```

This approach creates an isolated environment and a file Pipfile which documents dependencies, facilitating reproducibility.

Recommended tools (IDE, editors, terminal)

The choice of development tool directly impacts productivity. Modern code editors offer features such as syntax highlighting, auto-completion, debugging integration, and built-in terminals.

Visual Studio Code is a popular option due to its lightweight and extension support. Installing the official Python extension enables advanced functionality such as IntelliSense and debugging support.

```bash
code .
```

PyCharm is a complete IDE, offering native support for Python projects, integration with virtual environments, and an advanced code analysis system.

For users who prefer minimalist editors, **Neo's** and **Why** offer extreme customization with Python plugins.

In addition to the editor, the terminal plays a fundamental role. Consoles like Windows Terminal and iTerm2 provide a more fluid experience, while session managers like don't sleep allow the execution of multiple processes simultaneously.

Good initial configuration practices

The structuring of the environment influences the organization and scalability of the project. Well-structured projects use Git repositories for code versioning, ensuring traceability and efficient collaboration.

Initializing a repository:

```bash
git init
```

Auxiliary files such as .gitignore, must be configured to avoid versioning unnecessary files, such as installed dependencies.

Example of .gitignore for a Python project:

```csharp
__pycache__/
*.pyc
venv/
Pipfile.lock
```

Dependency managers must be used to maintain a controlled environment. With poetry, a project can be initialized and its dependencies managed with greater control:

bash

```
poetry init
poetry add flask fastapi
```

Linters and code formatters ensure code standardization and readability. Tools like flake8, black and isort help in writing clean and standardized code.

bash

```
pip install flake8 black isort
black .
isort .
flake8.
```

By setting up a well-structured development environment, application development with Flask and FastAPI becomes more efficient, avoiding problems and optimizing the workflow.

CHAPTER 3. PYTHON FOR WEB FUNDAMENTALS

Python stands out in web development due to its clear and objective syntax. To build efficient applications, understanding the fundamentals of the language is essential. Clean, readable code reduces errors and improves maintainability.

You **data types** are fundamental for manipulating information. Main categories include:

- **Numbers:** int, float, complex
- **Text:** str
- **Lists and tuples:** list, tuple
- **Sets and dictionaries:** set, dict
- **Booleanos:** bool

The assignment of variables follows a dynamic model:

python

```python
name = "Flask Web App"
version = 1.0
is_active = True
```

Python allows efficient manipulation of **strings**:

python

```python
message = "Web Development with Python"
print(message.lower())  # web development with python
print(message.upper())  # WEB DEVELOPMENT WITH PYTHON
```

```python
print(message.replace("Python", "FastAPI")) # Web
Development with FastAPI
```

The use of **f-strings** makes it easy to concatenate dynamic values:

python

```python
framework = "Flask"
print(f"Developing web applications with {framework}")
```

Data control and manipulation structures

Decision making and flow control are fundamental to web application logic.

The structure if-elif-else allows conditional code execution:

python

```python
user_role = "admin"

if user_role == "admin":
    print("Access granted")
elif user_role == "editor":
    print("Limited access")
else:
    print("Access denied")
```

THE **loop for** is widely used to traverse collections of data:

python

```python
users = ["Alice", "Bob", "Charlie"]

for user in users:
    print(f"Welcome, {user}!")
```

The function range() assists in controlled iteration:

python

```
for i in range(1, 6):
    print(f"Processing request {i}")
```

THE **loop while** executes code as long as the condition remains true:

python

```
count = 0

while count < 5:
    print(f"Attempt {count}")
    count += 1
```

The manipulation of **lists and dictionaries** is essential for storing and processing dynamic data:

python

```
tasks = ["Initialize server", "Connect to database", "Render templates"]
tasks.append("Handle user requests")

print(tasks)  # ['Initialize server', 'Connect to database', 'Render templates', 'Handle user requests']
```

Dictionaries allow key-value mapping:

python

```
user_info = {"name": "Alice", "role": "admin", "active": True}

print(user_info["name"])  # Alice
```

Function structuring modularizes code and improves reusability:

python

```python
def greet_user(name):
    return f"Hello, {name}!"

print(greet_user("Alice"))
```

Organization of modules and packages

Modularization allows large applications to be organized in a clear and scalable way. Python allows you to divide code into distinct files, promoting reuse and maintainability.

One **module** is any Python file (.py) that contains reusable functions or classes. Import can be done directly:

python

```python
import math

print(math.sqrt(16))  # 4.0
```

Custom modules can be created to structure code. Suppose a file helpers.py:

python

```python
def format_message(message):
    return message.upper()
```

Importing into another file makes the function available:

python

```python
from helpers import format_message

print(format_message("flask app initialized"))  # FLASK APP INITIALIZED
```

Packages group multiple modules into an organized structure.

A package is identified by a directory containing a file
__init__.py.

plaintext

```
app/
|— main.py
|— utils/
|   |— __init__.py
|   |— db.py
|   |— security.py
```

No module db.py:

python

```
def connect():
    return "Database connected"
```

No main.py, package import makes organization easier:

python

```
from utils.db import connect

print(connect())  # Database connected
```

Coding and readability standards

Well-structured code reduces complexity and facilitates
collaboration between developers. The PEP 8 guide defines best
practices for writing clean, readable code.

Variable and function names must be descriptive:

python

```
user_count = 100
def get_active_users():
    return user_count
```

Consistent indentation prevents errors and improves organization. Python uses four spaces for each indentation level:

python

```
def process_request(request):
    if request:
        print("Processing request")
```

Lines should not exceed 79 characters to facilitate reading on different screens. For long stretches, it is possible to use \ for line break:

python

```
message = "This is a long message that needs to be split " \
        "to improve readability in the code editor."
```

The use of **type hints** improves code clarity, facilitating maintenance and reducing errors:

python

```
def add_numbers(a: int, b: int) -> int:
    return a + b
```

Comments should be used to clarify critical sections, without redundancy:

python

```
# Hashing password before storing in the database
hashed_password = hash_function(user_password)
```

The adoption of automatic formatters, such as black, ensures standardization:

bash

```
pip install black
black app.py
```

Style checkers like flake8 identify inconsistencies:

bash

```
pip install flake8
flake8 app.py
```

Applying these principles improves efficiency in web development with Python, making code more reliable, readable, and scalable.

CHAPTER 4. HTTP CONCEPTS AND RESTFUL APIS

Communication between clients and servers on the web is based on a request-response model. The client sends a request, and the server returns a response containing the requested data or an error message. HTTP (Hypertext Transfer Protocol) emerged as the protocol underlying this model, facilitating the exchange of information between browsers and servers around the world. It is an application protocol that establishes how messages should be formatted and transmitted, influencing the way services and applications communicate.

The client-server architecture defines clear roles. The client, usually a browser or other application, initiates the request. The server, which receives the request, processes the information and sends an appropriate response. This division creates a scalable model, where multiple clients can interact with a server without needing to maintain a continuous connection.

HTTP works on top of TCP/IP, relying on lower layers to ensure that messages travel correctly across the network. HTTP messages contain headers that describe transmission details, such as content type, data size, and cache parameters, in addition to the body that carries the main content. Common headers include Host, User-Agent, Accept, Content-Type, and Content-Length. This flexibility facilitates the continued evolution of the protocol and the adoption of new media types.

The evolution of HTTP is linked to performance and security improvements. Later versions brought significant changes, such as HTTP/2 and HTTP/3, which introduced header compression techniques, request multiplexing and lower latency. This continuous evolution meets the demands of modern applications, which require fast and scalable responses.

Developers have the freedom to send and receive data in different formats. JSON (JavaScript Object Notation) has become a favorite in modern APIs as it combines lightness and readability. XML still appears in legacy services or specific integrations, while HTML is more common in pages rendered for end users.

HTTP Methods and Status Codes

The protocol defines methods (or verbs) that describe the intent of each request. The basic methods are GET, POST, PUT, DELETE, PATCH, HEAD and OPTIONS. Each has a specific purpose and semantics, allowing clients to clearly express the type of operation desired on the server.

GET obtains information without changing the server state. A GET request should not have side effects, such as inserting or modifying data, making it ideal for simple reading. An example of a GET request with the requests library in Python:

python

```python
import requests

response = requests.get("https://api.example.com/users")
if response.status_code == 200:
    data = response.json()
    print(data)
```

POST inserts or sends data to the server. This method is often used to create resources, such as adding a record to a database. A simple Python script:

python

```python
import requests

new_user = {
    "name": "Alice",
    "email": "alice@example.com"
}

response = requests.post("https://api.example.com/users",
json=new_user)
print(response.status_code)
```

PUT completely updates existing resources, replacing the previous representation with the sent data. DELETE removes existing resources. PATCH only updates specific fields on a resource. HEAD is similar to GET, but does not return the body. OPTIONS allows the client to know which methods and interactions the server accepts.

Status codes tell you whether the operation was successful or encountered a problem. Each code is divided into classes: 1xx (informational), 2xx (success), 3xx (redirections), 4xx (client errors) and 5xx (server errors). Correct use of these codes helps clients and developers understand the state of the request.

The 2xx category indicates success. 200 OK confirms that the request was processed without problems, while 201 Created signals that a new resource was created successfully. The 4xx category points out that there was an error on the client side. 400 Bad Request indicates a malformed request, 401 Unauthorized indicates authentication failures and 404 Not Found warns that the requested resource does not exist. The 5xx category represents server errors. The 500 Internal Server Error happens when the server encounters an internal problem, 503 Service Unavailable reports temporary unavailability.

Consistent adoption of these codes and methods brings

clarity, allowing clients to adapt and handle each situation appropriately. Systems that follow this approach become more predictable and easier to maintain.

RESTful API Principles

RESTful (Representational State Transfer) APIs are based on a set of principles that guarantee scalability, simplicity and flexibility. These principles include:

1. **Client-server architecture**
   The responsibility for presenting data to the user lies with the client, while the server manages storage and processing. This separation promotes greater organization and reuse of components.

2. **Interface uniforme**
   Communication between client and server follows resource, method and data formatting conventions. Each resource is accessed by a URI (Uniform Resource Identifier) and manipulated by HTTP methods, which brings predictability.

3. **Stateless**
   Each request is treated as independent. The server does not store client state, which facilitates horizontal scalability. If the user needs session information, the client sends tokens or credentials with each request.

4. **Cacheable**
   Responses can be marked as cacheable, improving performance and reducing network traffic. Headers like Cache-Control and ETag determine caching rules.

5. **Layered system**
   The architecture may include proxies, load balancers or other intermediate layers that ensure security, performance and scalability without changing the application logic.

6. **Code on demand (optional)**

This possibility allows the server to provide executable code to the client. In many cases, JavaScript is sent to the browser, making applications more dynamic.

To build robust RESTful APIs, it is common to represent resources with plural nouns. A route like /users represents the collection of users, while /users/{id} references a specific user. This pattern ensures predictability and makes it easier to understand what the route represents.

An example of a basic route in Flask to return all users:

python

```python
from flask import Flask, jsonify

app = Flask(__name__)

users = [
    {"id": 1, "name": "Alice"},
    {"id": 2, "name": "Bob"}
]

@app.route("/users", methods=["GET"])
def get_users():
    return jsonify(users)

if __name__ == "__main__":
    app.run(debug=True)
```

The GET method is applied to retrieve information. The response contains an array in JSON format with the desired information. This implementation reflects the REST guidelines: use of a method consistent with the intended action, resource representation through a plural noun and data return in a standardized format.

Comparison with other API architectures

The popularization of REST is due to its simplicity and adherence to the HTTP protocol. However, different architectures have emerged that meet specific demands. GraphQL, for example, offers a query language that allows customers to specify exactly what data they want to receive. Flexibility avoids data overload (over-fetching) and limits redundant requests (under-fetching), but requires a server that interprets and resolves queries dynamically. This model is useful for complex applications with multiple data views.

There are solutions based on RPC (Remote Procedure Call), where interactions resemble remote function calls. This style is popular in distributed systems that value the simplicity of integrating microservices. In contrast, REST resource semantics, with well-defined HTTP methods, are usually clearer for external integrations.

Some companies adopt the SOAP (Simple Object Access Protocol) standard in legacy corporate integrations. SOAP relies on XML and schemas for validating and describing services. Although it is robust, it is considered more complex and cumbersome compared to REST and JSON.

Event-based APIs are also gaining ground, especially when there is a need for real-time communication. Protocols like WebSockets allow for persistent connections, where server and client can continually exchange messages. This model fits into chat applications, streaming or monitoring dashboards.

REST maintains relevance by establishing simple conventions that intuitively use HTTP resources and methods. Many services and libraries optimize this interaction, and frameworks like Flask and FastAPI make it easy to create endpoints following these practices. The choice of other architectures depends on the scenario, but REST remains the dominant approach as it balances simplicity, scalability and robustness.

RESTful APIs encourage developers to explore the pattern of well-defined resources and endpoints that convey clear meaning. The success of an API also depends on good documentation and versioning practices, as external integrations require precise instructions and stability throughout the application lifecycle. Tools like OpenAPI (Swagger) automate this process, generating interactive documentation based on the routes defined in the code.

In many projects, REST APIs serve as a gateway to more complex systems. Frontend applications, internal microservices and even IoT devices can communicate with these endpoints, becoming part of a scalable and interoperable ecosystem. The HTTP protocol, combined with methods and status codes, creates a clear dialogue between components that can be distributed globally. This scenario drives the adoption of REST as the main communication standard between different platforms.

The evolution of web development and the high demand for integrations keep REST in the spotlight, as many development tools provide out-of-the-box support. The large volume of resources available, such as libraries and articles, makes it possible to quickly adopt this architecture. The community also provides feedback and best practices for dealing with security, versioning, authentication, and other needs that arise when building mature APIs.

When a team decides between REST, GraphQL, gRPC or SOAP, several factors are evaluated: scalability, team familiarity with the standard, performance needs and version requirements. REST remains a safe choice in numerous situations. Despite the community increasingly exploring GraphQL, and gRPC attracting projects that value high speed in internal communications, REST is still the first option in many integration projects between services and legacy systems.

Adopting REST does not prevent combinations with other

styles. A solution might expose a REST endpoint to external clients, while internally using a different protocol for critical services. This hybrid model allows you to take advantage of the popularity and capabilities of REST together with the advantages of another standard in internal communications.

The most important thing is to maintain consistency in the way you define routes and resources, document each endpoint and adopt methods and status codes correctly. Standardization avoids confusion and rework, especially when multiple developers collaborate on the same project or when new teams take over system maintenance.

These concepts form the foundation of modern applications, guiding the way clients and servers interact. HTTP establishes the data transport mechanism, methods and status codes define the behavior of requests, and REST organizes the rules for accessing resources. Understanding these elements allows you to create resilient, scalable solutions that follow good web development practices. When these solutions grow, integrations with third parties become simpler, as many companies expect APIs to follow market standards. This reduces adoption barriers and accelerates the construction of increasingly complex digital ecosystems.

Projects that follow this model are more likely to be successful in the long term, as the community and monitoring and documentation tools are widespread, offering support and enabling continuous improvements. Therefore, mastering the fundamentals of HTTP, methods, status codes, and REST creates a solid foundation for moving forward in creating robust and reliable APIs.

CHAPTER 5. INTRODUCTION TO FLASK

Flask emerged in the Python ecosystem as a project that prioritizes simplicity and freedom of choice when building web applications. The initiative came from Armin Ronacher and members of the Pocoo community, who sought to create a lean base, without structural impositions, but which still offered the power to expand through extensions. The project was created based on an experiment called Denied, a joke on April Fools' Day, which ended up evolving into something serious when it became evident that there was a need for a minimalist microframework for Python.

The core idea is based on providing only the essentials to start a web application, leaving each developer to decide which additional libraries are appropriate. This choice contrasts with other frameworks that adopt more complete and opinionated approaches, inserting internal tools for each part of development. In Flask, programmer autonomy allows you to integrate specific database solutions, authentication, templates or other functionalities, without being tied to a monolithic package.

The community quickly adopted this philosophy as it combines lightness and flexibility. Many start with a simple Python script, adding pieces as the application grows. This mentality appeals to those who prefer full control over each dependency and do not want to learn the rules of a complex framework. Flask embraces practices from the Python ecosystem, encouraging modularization, use of virtual environments, and adoption of coding standards to keep the application clean and sustainable.

This origin story highlights the experimental and collaborative nature of the open source ecosystem, as the game has become one of the most popular solutions for web development in Python. The minimalist philosophy remains today, attracting both beginners who want to take their first steps, and professionals who need total architectural freedom.

Advantages of the micro framework

The concept of micro framework refers to the proposal to offer only minimal functionalities to deal with routes, requests and responses, without including database tools, template systems or authentication modules. Many advantages arise from this approach:

- **Reduced learning curve**
  Few internal concepts make the framework simpler to understand. Beginners can grasp the basics quickly, building APIs and web servers without knowledge overload.
- **Flexibility in choosing extensions**
  The absence of pre-built solutions leaves room for each project to use its preferred libraries. It is possible to adopt SQLAlchemy, MongoEngine or another ORM for data persistence, as well as implement different authentication strategies according to the application's needs.
- **Easy maintenance**
  A small, well-segmented codebase makes updates and troubleshooting easier. The lean structure makes code reading faster, as each additional dependency is chosen consciously and follows a clear purpose.
- **Community and support**
  Flask has remained popular for years, which has resulted in a wide variety of tutorials, extensions, and examples available in public repositories. The vast community

shares best practices for security, scalability, and integration with external services.

- **Gradual scalability**
  Applications started simply can grow without rewriting everything. Those who need more features add modules and libraries as the application expands.

These points make Flask attractive for rapid prototyping, RESTful APIs, internal administration systems, and even large applications that benefit from the flexible architecture. The decision to use a micro framework is often based on personal preferences, project size, and customization requirements.

Installation and first steps

Flask requires Python installed in an up-to-date version. Creating a virtual environment often ensures that dependencies are isolated. Following the good practices mentioned in previous topics, it is common to start like this:

bash

```
python -m venv venv
source venv/bin/activate  # Linux/macOS
venv\Scripts\activate.bat # Windows
```

With the virtual environment active, installation is done via pip:

bash

```
pip install flask
```

The first project usually starts with a file that defines basic routes. Many name this file as app.py or main.py. An example of a minimal application:

python

```
# EXAMPLE 1
# STEP 1: importing the Flask class and jsonify function
from flask import Flask, jsonify

# STEP 2: Flask instance creation
app = Flask(__name__)

# STEP 3: Defining a simple route that returns a JSON response
@app.route("/")
def home():
    return jsonify(message="Hello Flask")

# STEP 4: running the server in debug mode for development
if __name__ == "__main__":
    app.run(debug=True)
# FINALIZATION
```

In the above script, the method route binds the root path ("/")
to the function home. When a client accesses this endpoint,
the response returns a JSON object with the message. The
function run starts the local server.

Common Mistakes and How to Fix Them

- **Common Error**: ModuleNotFoundError: No module
  named 'flask'
  Error Message: This error usually appears when Flask
  has not been installed in the correct environment or the
  virtual environment is not activated.
  Probable Cause: Lack of activation of the virtual
  environment or installation outside the virtual
  environment.
  Correct Solution: Activate the virtual environment and
  install Flask again.
- **Common Error**: NameError: name 'Flask' is not defined
  Error Message: Python does not recognize the Flask class.
  Probable Cause: Missing import or typing error in the

class name.

Correct Solution: Check if the line from flask import Flask is present and that the name is written correctly.

- **Common Error**: OSError: [Errno 98] Address already in use

  Error Message: The port used by Flask is busy.

  Probable Cause: Another process is listening on the same port (usually 5000).

  Correct Solution: End the running process or change the port, for example: app.run(debug=True, port=5001).

Basic structure of a Flask application

Simplicity allows you to start with a single file, but it is common to reorganize the application into multiple modules as it grows. A typical structure:

plaintext

```
my_flask_app/
├── app.py
├── requirements.txt
├── config.py
├── static/
│   └── styles.css
├── templates/
│   └── index.html
└── .gitignore
```

Each element plays a role:

- app.py contains the main routes and initial logic.
- requirements.txt lists dependencies, allowing other developers to replicate the environment.
- config.py can store sensitive settings such as database credentials or API keys.
- pasta static/ houses static files such as CSS, images, and JavaScript.

- pasta templates/ stores HTML files, processed by Flask's template engine (Jinja2).

An example with additional routes and use of templates:

python

```python
# EXAMPLE 2
# STEP 1: importing Flask and render_template
from flask import Flask, render_template

app = Flask(__name__)

# STEP 2: route to the home page, returning an HTML template
@app.route("/")
def index():
    return render_template("index.html")

# STEP 3: Route to display details of a user, using route
parameters
@app.route("/user/<username>")
def show_user(username):
    return f"User Profile: {username}"

# STEP 4: running in debug mode
if __name__ == "__main__":
    app.run(debug=True)
# FINALIZATION
```

THE render_template uses Jinja2, a templating engine that allows you to create dynamic pages. The file index.html (within templates/) could it be:

html

```html
<!-- index.html -->
<!DOCTYPE html>
<html>
<head>
```

```
  <meta charset="utf-8">
  <title>Flask App</title>
</head>
<body>
  <h1>Welcome to Flask!</h1>
</body>
</html>
```

Flask, by default, looks for templates in the folder templates. You can customize this path if necessary. When the route / is accessed, the function index party render_template("index.html"), returning the HTML to the browser.

Common Mistakes and How to Fix Them

- **Common Error**: jinja2.exceptions.TemplateNotFound: index.html
  Error Message: Flask does not find the requested template file.
  Probable Cause: File outside directory templates or incorrect name.
  Correct Solution: Confirm that index.html is in the folder templates and that the file name matches the one passed to render_template.
- **Common Error**: TypeError: 'NoneType' object is not callable
  Error Message: Normally occurs if the function render_template was not imported correctly or was overwritten.
  Probable Cause: Import failed: from flask import render_template.
  Correct Solution: Ensure import and check that there is no variable or function named as render_template.

Code Formatting and Structure

Flask supports the organization of code into modules, avoiding concentration of logic in a single file. In larger projects, creating a folder app/ with several submodules improves encapsulation:

plaintext

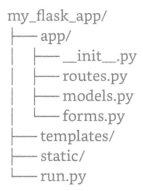

```
my_flask_app/
├── app/
│   ├── __init__.py
│   ├── routes.py
│   ├── models.py
│   └── forms.py
├── templates/
├── static/
└── run.py
```

A file __init__.py inside app/ initializes the application and registers routes:

python

```python
# EXAMPLE 3
# STEP 1: importing Flask and creating the instance
from flask import Flask

def create_app():
    app = Flask(__name__)

    # Application settings
    app.config["SECRET_KEY"] = "any-random-secret-key"

    # Registering routes
    from app.routes import main
    app.register_blueprint(main)

    return app
# FINALIZATION
```

No routes.py:

python

```python
# EXAMPLE 4
# STEP 1: Importing Blueprint
from flask import Blueprint, jsonify

main = Blueprint("main", __name__)

# STEP 2: defining routes within the Blueprint
@main.route("/")
def index():
    return jsonify(message="Blueprint routing works")
# FINALIZATION
```

No run.py:

python

```python
# EXAMPLE 5
# STEP 1: importing the create_app function
from app import create_app

# STEP 2: instantiating the application
app = create_app()

# STEP 3: running the application
if __name__ == "__main__":
    app.run(debug=True)
# FINALIZATION
```

This form of organization makes it easier to separate routes, models and forms into separate files, keeping the project clean. THE Blueprint is a powerful feature that helps modularize large applications. Each module can register its routes and configuration, and they are all integrated into the main file that starts the server.

Common Mistakes and How to Fix Them

- **Common Error:** ImportError: cannot import name 'main' from partially initialized module 'app.routes'
  Error Message: Python was unable to resolve the dependency between modules.
  Probable Cause: Circular import or incorrect hierarchy.
  Correct Solution: Check if app.routes not importing something app.__init__ which generates reciprocal dependence. Adjust the order of imports and separation of functions.
- **Common Error:** KeyError: 'SECRET_KEY'
  Error Message: A configuration key that does not exist was accessed.
  Probable Cause: Lack of definition of the SECRET_KEY or typing error.
  Correct Solution: Ensure configuration app.config["SECRET_KEY"] = "some_key" or check the name used during access.

Highlight of good practices

Flask offers flexibility, but adopting certain practices strengthens the application:

- **Blueprints** to modularize broken
- **Good folder organization** to not overload a single file
- **Dependency Management** through a file requirements.txt or Pipfile
- **Environment variables** to keep secrets and keys out of source code
- **Using Linters** like flake8 and formatters like black to standardize the style

Segmented codes make it easier to understand each part of the project. Comments should be objective, describing the motivation for code snippets. Avoid redundant comments to maintain reading fluidity.

Flask enables a quick, unblockable start, offering a robust structure for those who need freedom and progressive growth. The minimalist philosophy directs the developer to make conscious architectural decisions. Those who embrace this microframework have access to an extensive community, as well as a rich set of extensions that cover areas such as security, databases and authentication.

The transition from a simple prototype to a large-scale project happens organically, thanks to modularization and the ability to integrate custom tools. From these foundations, highly specialized applications can emerge, ready to serve business niches or more general projects, such as APIs, backend services or even administration systems. This flexibility explains Flask's constant popularity among teams that value speed and autonomy when designing web solutions.

CHAPTER 6. STRUCTURE AND ROUTING IN FLASK

Configuring routes and managing the flow of requests is one of the central points in any web application, especially in projects that use Flask to structure API endpoints or HTML pages. Routing allows you to control how the server responds to specific requests by defining the logic for each URL and directing users to the appropriate resources. An application with well-organized routes tends to be easier to maintain, as the relationship between each address and the associated functionality is clear. Routes form the basis for creating RESTful services, integrations with frontends, and even internal communications between microservices. Flask is known for its simplicity when establishing these paths, as it adopts a system of decorators that makes the code more readable.

There is flexibility to model routes according to each team's preferences, offering freedom to use dynamic variables, different treatment of HTTP methods and, when necessary, organization into multiple modules. The way each route is configured impacts user experience and application clarity, as good endpoint names help communicate the purpose of each resource. Using route parameters makes it easier to create paths that reflect unique identities, such as user IDs or category names, without having to resort to query strings for simple information.

This process covers the layers of configuration, creation and mapping of endpoints, as well as the handling of dynamic parameters. The approach adopted by Flask concentrates these definitions in decorators, making the code flow clear. In larger projects, modular organization takes center stage, since concentrating routing logic in a single file can make future maintenance difficult. The combination of Blueprints and good architectural practices allows you to scale the application without sacrificing readability.

This session covers the definition of routes, the use of decorators, the manipulation of dynamic variables and the best way to structure routing so that the project's growth is sustained. Examples are presented in Python that can be adapted according to the needs of each application. Whenever a script is presented, troubleshooting sections are included to help identify common problems and resolve them quickly.

Route configuration and definition

Flask uses the concept of routing to associate URLs with Python functions responsible for generating responses. When a client makes a request for a given path, the Flask server finds the corresponding route and executes the linked function. In simple configurations, just a few lines of code are enough to establish initial routes and verify the application's functionality.

A main file that illustrates route creation can be called app.py:

python

```python
# EXAMPLE 1
# STEP 1: Importing required modules
from flask import Flask, jsonify, request

# STEP 2: Launching the Flask application
app = Flask(__name__)

# STEP 3: route definition for the root path
@app.route("/", methods=["GET"])
def home():
```

```
    return jsonify(message="Welcome to the home page")

# STEP 4: Route to an information endpoint
@app.route("/info", methods=["GET"])
def info():
    return jsonify(app_name="MyFlaskApp", version="1.0")

# STEP 5: running the server in debug mode
if __name__ == "__main__":
    app.run(debug=True)
# FINALIZATION
```

This script creates two routes. The first corresponds to the root path "/" and responds only to the GET method with a JSON message. The second, in "/info", returns additional information about the application. Each route is associated with a Python function that performs specific tasks. If the server is running on the default port (5000), access http://127.0.0.1:5000/info will show the JSON object defined by the function info.

Common Errors and How to Fix Them:

- **Common Error:** TypeError: 'NoneType' object is not callable
  Error Message: Generally indicates that some decorator was not imported or was overwritten.
  Probable Cause: Lack of import app.route or incorrect use of decorators.
  Correct Solution: Ensure that from flask import Flask and the correct use of @app.route(...). Check if app it was not subsequently reset.
- **Common Error:** RuntimeError: Working outside of request context
  Error Message: Flask does not recognize the request context during an operation that depends on that context.

Probable Cause: Function that accesses request objects (request, session) outside the route flow.

Correct Solution: Perform these operations within the function associated with the decorator, avoiding out-of-context calls.

- **Common Error:** Method Not Allowed (405)

Error Message: The route was accessed with a different HTTP method than the one configured.

Probable Cause: Absence of methods=["GET", "POST"] or invalid method.

Correct Solution: Include all allowed methods in the decorator.

Using decorators for endpoint mapping

Flask stands out for adopting decorators to map routes declaratively. Instead of recording each path in a route table manually, simply annotate the functions with decorator @app.route("/path", methods=["..."]) to associate them with the corresponding endpoint. This style makes it easier to read, as the route and function are close together, avoiding searches in different parts of the code.

When HTTP methods are omitted, the default is GET. In projects that require resource creation, POST is often enabled. For update, PUT or PATCH can be specified, while DELETE removes data. Annotating appropriate methods makes the API clearer while also following RESTful practices.

An example route to create an item in the database via POST:

python

```
# EXAMPLE 2
# STEP 1: importing modules
from flask import Flask, request, jsonify

app = Flask(__name__)
```

```
# STEP 2: route that accepts POST to create a resource
@app.route("/items", methods=["POST"])
def create_item():
    data = request.get_json()
    item_name = data.get("name")
    item_value = data.get("value")

    # Persistence logic in bank or memory
    new_item = {"id": 123, "name": item_name, "value":
item_value}

    return jsonify(new_item), 201

if __name__ == "__main__":
    app.run(debug=True)
# FINALIZATION
```

The decorator has @app.route("/items", methods=["POST"]) to register the function create_item. When sending POST requests to /items, this code extracts data from the request body via request.get_json(), creates an object, returns it in JSON with status 201 (Created). This flow exemplifies the recommended approach in an API that follows REST practices, as the plural path of /items suggests creating multiple items.

Common Errors and How to Fix Them:

- Common Error: KeyError when accessing data["name"]
  Error Message: Indicates that the key "name" is not present in the data.
  Probable Cause: Request body does not have this field.
  Correct Solution: Use data.get("name") to avoid KeyError. Verify that the client is sending valid JSON.
- Common Error: 400 Bad Request when calling the route
  Error Message: The server does not understand the request.
  Probable Cause: The client may be sending data in an

incorrect format or without proper headers, such as
Content-Type: application/json.
Correct Solution: Check the request format and header.
- Common Error: Lack of JSON return and status code
  Error Message: In logs, you may notice that the route is
  not returning the desired response.
  Probable Cause: The function does not end with return
  jsonify(...).
  Correct Solution: Ensure data conversion into
  appropriate JSON and status code.

Route parameters and dynamic variables

Applications often receive parameters that identify specific
resources. A user ID, for example, can be part of the URL,
helping to maintain routes without excessive query strings.
Flask allows you to define routes with dynamic variables using
syntax <type:variable>. The type can be int, float, path, or
omitted for strings.

Example route that gets an item by ID:

python

```
# EXAMPLE 3
# STEP 1: route with integer route parameter
@app.route("/items/<int:item_id>", methods=["GET"])
def get_item(item_id):
    # Retrieve item by ID from a database
    # If found, return it
    sample_item = {"id": item_id, "name": "SampleItem", "value":
99}

    return jsonify(sample_item), 200
# FINALIZATION
```

The route /items/<int:item_id> captures the value as an
integer, storing it in the variable item_id. If the customer

requests /items/10, the function receives item_id=10. If the type is omitted, the value will be interpreted as a string. In case of <path:some_path>, you can capture additional bars.

Common Errors and How to Fix Them:

- Common Error: Not Found when accessing /items/text
  Error Message: The route does not accept strings for item_id, as it was declared with <int:item_id>.
  Probable Cause: The defined path only accepts integers.
  Correct Solution: Switch to <string:item_id> or <item_id> if the intention is to capture non-numeric values.

- Common Error: Type conversion failed
  Error Message: May occur if <int:item_id> is used, but the value received is not a valid number.
  Probable Cause: The URL contained non-numeric characters.
  Correct Solution: Check if the client sends correct values. Adjust the route if necessary.

Modular organization of routes

Larger applications benefit from dividing routing into different modules. Placing all routes in the same app.py file can become unfeasible over time, as it makes maintenance and understanding difficult. Flask offers Blueprints, which allow you to group related routes into a single component, favoring modularization.

A project can have the following structure:

markdown

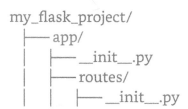

```
my_flask_project/
├── app/
│   ├── __init__.py
│   ├── routes/
│   │   ├── __init__.py
```

```
|   |     ┌── items.py
|   |     └── users.py
|   └── extensions/
|       └── __init__.py
├── run.py
├── requirements.txt
└── ...
```

In the archive items.py:

python

```python
# EXAMPLE 4
# STEP 1: importing modules
from flask import Blueprint, jsonify, request

items_bp = Blueprint("items_bp", __name__)

# STEP 2: route to get all items
@items_bp.route("/items", methods=["GET"])
def list_items():
    sample_items = [
        {"id": 1, "name": "Book", "value": 30},
        {"id": 2, "name": "Laptop", "value": 1500}
    ]
    return jsonify(sample_items), 200

# STEP 3: route to create item
@items_bp.route("/items", methods=["POST"])
def create_item():
    data = request.get_json()
    name = data.get("name")
    value = data.get("value")
    new_item = {"id": 3, "name": name, "value": value}
    return jsonify(new_item), 201
# FINALIZATION
```

No users.py:

python

```python
# EXAMPLE 5
# STEP 1: importing modules
from flask import Blueprint, jsonify

users_bp = Blueprint("users_bp", __name__)

# STEP 2: Route to get user details
@users_bp.route("/users/<int:user_id>", methods=["GET"])
def get_user(user_id):
    user_info = {"id": user_id, "name": "User Example", "role": "admin"}
    return jsonify(user_info), 200
# FINALIZATION
```

No __init__.py **inside** routes/:

python

```python
# EXAMPLE 6
# STEP 1: importing the Blueprints
from .items import items_bp
from .users import users_bp

# The __all__ variable can be used to publicly export objects
__all__ = ["items_bp", "users_bp"]
# FINALIZATION
```

No app/__init__.py:

python

```python
# EXAMPLE 7
# STEP 1: importing Flask and Blueprints
```

```
from flask import Flask
from app.routes import items_bp, users_bp

def create_app():
    app = Flask(__name__)

    # STEP 2: registration of Blueprints
    app.register_blueprint(items_bp)
    app.register_blueprint(users_bp)

    return app
# FINALIZATION
```

No run.py:

python

```
# EXAMPLE 8
# STEP 1: Importing create_app
from app import create_app

app = create_app()

if __name__ == "__main__":
    app.run(debug=True)
# FINALIZATION
```

When starting the server with python run.py, the routes defined in items.py and users.py become active. The endpoints /items and /users/<int:user_id> respond according to the established logic. Modularization increases clarity as each module groups routes with similar responsibility. In large applications, it is common to include subfolders to organize each macrofunctionality or business area, in addition to dividing route code, domain logic, data models and validations.

Common Errors and How to Fix Them:

- **Common Error:** ImportError: cannot import name 'items_bp' from 'app.routes'
  Error Message: Indicates that the module items_bp was not found in app.routes.
  Probable Cause: Lack of correct import in the __init__.py of routes.
  Correct Solution: Check if from .items import items_bp is present not __init__.py and if the file items.py exists.
- **Common Error:** AssertionError: View function mapping is overwriting an existing endpoint function
  Error Message: Flask detected that two routes use the same function or endpoint name.
  Probable Cause: Duplicate decorators or endpoints that have the same URL and internal name.
  Correct Solution: Adjust function names or paths. Can be used endpoint='unique_name' to differentiate explicitly.
- **Common Error:** ValueError: View function did not return a response
  Error Message: The function associated with the decorator returned nothing.
  Probable Cause: Lack of return on some silent condition or exception.
  Correct Solution: Ensure that the function returns an answer in all execution paths.

A solid set of routes facilitates collaboration, as each developer understands the function of each endpoint, its parameters, and which payload is expected or returned. Flask stands out for simplifying the definition of these paths, using decorators that combine readability with expressiveness. In projects that grow quickly, maintaining a single route file tends to create confusion and hinder evolution, making the modular approach the ideal choice for corporate or medium to large applications.

The use of route parameters makes the application more

intuitive, as it enriches the semantics of the paths and avoids polluting the body of requests with redundant data. Dynamic variables can be combined with different HTTP methods to implement REST patterns. Even without focusing solely on REST, this practice brings coherence to the architecture and makes URLs more predictable.

The advantages of well-planned routing appear in the maintenance phase. The programmer returning to a project after weeks or months quickly identifies the function of each route. The habit of creating Blueprints for each functional area reduces couplings, helping with versioning and continuous integration. Furthermore, route separation helps with the application of security and authorization at specific points, as each Blueprint can receive its own rules and middleware.

For teams that deal with multiple services, it is possible to integrate routes that communicate with external APIs. A Flask microservice can expose endpoints that connect to another system, storing or transforming data as needed. Modularization makes it possible to distribute functionalities without merging different codes into a single huge file. This pattern is especially advantageous when planning to scale the application, replacing parts of the system or integrating new modules without complete refactoring.

Routes in Flask are more than just paths. They are the link between users (or API clients) and the business logic that the application executes. When configured clearly, they help create a positive experience for those who use the service, in addition to making the work of those who develop it easier. The syntax based on decorators, combined with good modularization practices, forms a coherent set that covers everything from study projects to production applications.

Convention-driven routing, such as using plural names for collections (e.g. /products, /users), is already a standard in the Python ecosystem and other languages that adopt REST. This consistency improves communication between developers from different teams, as it is easy to identify the function of each endpoint without the need for extensive documentation. Whenever possible, combine the approach with automatic documentation tools, such as Swagger or another OpenAPI specification generator, providing updated documentation as routes are defined.

Choosing clear names for functions and paths, taking care to define appropriate methods, and correctly using HTTP status codes contribute to building well-structured APIs and applications. Flask, focused on simplicity, offers an environment conducive to this kind of clarity. Based on these bases, subsequent chapters and topics can explore more advanced Flask features, always on a consistent foundation of routing and organization, where each part of the application has a well-defined place, minimizing rework and optimizing the development team's day-to-day activities.

CHAPTER 7. TEMPLATES AND RENDERING WITH JINJA2

Jinja2 is the template engine that makes it possible to separate presentation logic from business logic, allowing the creation of dynamic and reusable layouts. The intuitive and flexible syntax makes it easy to insert variables, execute loops and conditionals directly in HTML files, without mixing Python code with markup. This mechanism allows you to develop complex and dynamic interfaces, integrating server data in an organized and elegant way. The template language adopts delimiters such as {{ variable }} to display values and {% ... %} for flow control, enabling the execution of conditional and iterative structures.

Jinja2 syntax uses variables, filters, and macros to transform and format data before presenting it. For example, when using a variable on a page, the content can be modified using filters to change the format, capitalization or apply custom functions. The conditional structure allows you to use {% if condition %} to determine which pieces of HTML should be rendered based on the data sent. Iterating over lists and dictionaries uses {% for item in items %} to dynamically generate elements. The clarity of these commands makes the maintenance and evolution of templates simpler, with code that approaches natural language, without mixing server logic with visual presentation.

Understanding the fundamentals of Jinja2 is essential to making the most of its potential. The language supports the definition of macros, which are reusable functions in templates, and allows the inclusion of other templates with

{% include "header.html" %} to create modular layouts. Filters, such as |capitalize or |date, transform data in a simple way, making it easier to adapt values to presentation needs. The language also makes it possible to create complex expressions using parentheses and logical operators, keeping the code clean and organized.

The organization of templates in a Flask project usually follows a standard structure, where all HTML files reside in a folder called templates, while static files, such as CSS and JavaScript, are in a separate folder, usually called static. This separation of concerns ensures that rendering logic is isolated from code and resource files, making the project more modular and easier to manage. The rendering flow goes through Flask, which, upon receiving a request, searches for the corresponding template, injects the necessary variables and sends the rendered response to the client.

Creating and organizing HTML templates involves defining the page structure and the points where dynamic data will be inserted. Each HTML file can have fixed and variable sections, and component reuse is facilitated with template inheritance. This technique allows you to define a base layout with standard sections, such as header, footer and sidebar, which will be extended by other templates that only specify different content for each page. The modular approach helps maintain visual consistency and makes maintenance easier, as changes to the base layout automatically propagate to all pages that inherit it.

The structuring of templates must consider the clarity and readability of the HTML code. Using consistent indentation and explanatory comments (succinctly) helps identify sections and blocks of code. The practice of separating components into smaller files, such as dividing the navigation bar into a separate file, allows you to include this component on multiple pages using the {% include "navbar.html" %}

command. This strategy avoids code duplication and makes changes simpler, as modifications to a single file update all pages that depend on it.

The template inheritance technique is essential to avoid redundancy and promote reuse. A base file, often called base.html, defines the overall structure of the page and contains blocks marked with {% block content %} and other identified blocks that will be replaced by the templates they inherit. The inheritance mechanism allows the child template to only redefine the necessary sections while keeping the main layout intact. This approach improves maintenance because changes to the base layout are automatically reflected in all derived pages.

The inclusion of templates, using the {% include "arquivo.html" %} command, makes it possible to divide the code into smaller components. Components such as footers, headers and forms can be developed separately and included in the main templates. This modularization facilitates collaboration in teams, as different developers can work on specific parts without affecting the whole. The use of macros, which function as functions, allows you to encapsulate repetitive rendering logic, receiving parameters and returning already formatted HTML snippets. Such features promote standardization and reduce code duplication, which is crucial for maintaining large-scale applications.

Flask uses Jinja2 as its templating engine natively. The render_template function is responsible for locating the HTML file in the templates folder, injecting the variables passed by the server and generating the final HTML to be sent to the client. Integration with Flask makes the rendering flow simple and transparent, where data obtained from databases or APIs can be passed directly to templates, allowing the creation of dynamic and responsive pages.

Below is an example of a template structure that can be

adapted according to the complexity of the project. Imagine a project with the following organization:

```
my_flask_app/
    ├── app.py
    ├── templates/
    │   ├── base.html
    │   ├── index.html
    │   ├── about.html
    │   └── components/
    │       ├── header.html
    │       └── footer.html
    └── static/
        ├── css/
        │   └── main.css
        └── js/
            └── main.js
```

The base.html file contains the structure common to all pages, with blocks defined for dynamic content. A snippet of base.html can be structured as follows:

html

```html
<!-- base.html -->
<!DOCTYPE html>
<html lang="yes">
<head>
    <meta charset="UTF-8">
    <meta name="viewport" content="width=device-width, initial-scale=1.0">
    <title>{% block title %}My Flask App{% endblock %}</title>
    <link rel="stylesheet" href="{{ url_for('static', filename='css/main.css') }}">
</head>
<body>
    {% include "components/header.html" %}
```

```
<div class="container">
    {% block content %}{% endblock %}
</div>
{% include "components/footer.html" %}
<script src="{{ url_for('static', filename='js/main.js') }}"></script>
</body>
</html>
```

In base.html, the HTML structure is defined with header, footer and main content area. The inclusion of the header.html and footer.html components promotes reuse, while the title and content blocks enable specific pages to customize content according to their needs.

The index.html file, which extends the base layout, defines the specific content of the home page. Using the extends command, the child template indicates that it inherits the entire structure of base.html, overwriting only the necessary blocks:

html

```
<!-- index.html -->
{% extends "base.html" %}
{% block title %}Home - My Flask App{% endblock %}
{% block content %}
    <h1>Welcome to My Flask App</h1>
    <p>This is the home page rendered using Jinja2
templates.</p>
    <ul>
      {% for item in items %}
        <li>{{ item }}</li>
      {% endfor %}
    </ul>
{% endblock %}
```

The about.html file can follow the same logic, defining information about the application:

html

```
<!-- about.html -->
{% extends "base.html" %}
{% block title %}About - My Flask App{% endblock %}
{% block content %}
    <h2>About Us</h2>
    <p>We build dynamic and responsive web applications
with Flask and Jinja2.</p>
{% endblock %}
```

The header and footer components are developed in a modular way for inclusion in different templates. The header.html can contain a simple navigation menu:

html

```
<!-- components/header.html -->
<header>
    <none>
      <ul>
        <li><a href="{{ url_for('index') }}">Home</a></li>
        <li><a href="{{ url_for('about') }}">About</a></li>
        <li><a href="{{ url_for('contact') }}">Contact</a></li>
      </ul>
    </none>
</header>
```

While footer.html may include copyright information and additional links:

html

```
<!-- components/footer.html -->
```

```
<footer>
    <p>&copy; 2025 My Flask App. All rights reserved.</p>
</footer>
```

The rendering of these templates is controlled by Flask. In the main file, the render_template function injects variables and selects the correct template for each route defined. A snippet of Python code illustrating the integration with Flask can be seen below:

python

```python
# EXAMPLE 1: app.py structure
from flask import Flask, render_template

app = Flask(__name__)

@app.route("/")
def index():
    items = ["Item A", "Item B", "Item C"]
    return render_template("index.html", items=items)

@app.route("/about")
def about():
    return render_template("about.html")

@app.route("/contact")
def contact():
    contact_details = {
        "email": "contact@myflaskapp.com",
        "phone": "+1-234-567-890"
    }
    return                      render_template("contact.html",
contact=contact_details)

if __name__ == "__main__":
    app.run(debug=True)
```

In the code above, the root route injects a list of items into the items variable, allowing the index.html template to iterate over this set and generate a dynamic list. The about route just calls render_template to load the content defined in about.html. The contact route can be configured in a similar way, with data passed to the template, which, in turn, displays the contact information.

Common problems when developing with Jinja2 can include template files not being found or syntax errors. Error messages like TemplateNotFound indicate that Flask was unable to find the specified file in the templates folder. It is recommended to check that the folder structure is correct and that the file name exactly matches that specified in the render_template function. Other errors can occur if delimiters are not closed correctly, generating syntax error messages. Ensuring that each opening {{ or {% tag has its corresponding closing tag is crucial to avoiding these failures.

Integration with variables and filters is another area of attention. The use of native filters, such as |upper, |lower or |capitalize, allows data to be transformed dynamically. For example, when displaying a username, you might use {{ username | Capitalize }} to ensure the first letter is capitalized. The creation of custom filters is also supported by Jinja2 and can be registered in Flask during application configuration, expanding the data formatting capacity.

Macro implementation allows you to create reusable blocks of code, such as forms or repetitive components. When defining a macro, the HTML code can be parameterized and included at different points in the template. For example, defining a macro to display an alert message can be done as follows in a separate file such as macros.html:

html

```
<!-- macros.html -->
{% macro alert(message, alert_type="info") -%}
<div class="alert alert-{{ alert_type }}">
    {{ message }}
</div>
{%- endmacro %}
```

The alert macro can be included in any template that needs to display messages, simply by importing the macro file:

html

```
{% import "macros.html" as macros %}
{{ macros.alert("Operation completed successfully",
"success") }}
```

This approach centralizes the logic for displaying alerts and facilitates future changes, as all you need to do is edit the macro file to modify the behavior on all pages that use it. Modularity is reinforced when macros and template components are divided into specific files, allowing for more efficient maintenance and a conflict-free collaborative development flow.

Using blocks for template inheritance creates a hierarchical relationship between files. The base file defines the global structure, while files that extend it only need to overwrite the blocks relevant to the specific page. For example, the area for main content is defined in the base file as {% block content %}...{% endblock %}. Templates that extend the base layout only need to provide content for this block, maintaining the visual and structural consistency of the application. This method reduces code duplication, as common elements, such as headers and footers, are defined once in the base layout and inherited across all pages.

Dynamic rendering with Jinja2 is powerful and flexible,

allowing complex data to be displayed in an organized way. Passing dictionaries, lists and objects directly to the template makes it possible to create interactive interfaces that adapt to server data. For example, when rendering a list of products, the template can iterate over each item and display information such as name, price, and description, using loops and conditionals to handle cases where the list is empty or contains null values.

Debugging tools can be useful during template development. Configuring Flask in debug mode displays detailed error messages on the screen, making it easier to identify problems in the syntax or logic of the templates. It is also recommended to use specific linters for HTML and Jinja2, which point out inconsistencies and formatting errors, contributing to the quality of the delivered code. The integration of automated tests that verify the rendering of templates with simulated data is another practice that helps to avoid regressions and unexpected failures in production.

Template management becomes even more relevant when working with applications that require customization for different devices or contexts. Using CSS and JavaScript integrated through the templating engine allows you to dynamically adjust the layout and behavior of the interface. Passing environment variables to templates makes it possible to change themes, logos or other visual properties without the need to change the source code, simply by modifying the parameters on the server.

The complexity of modern projects demands a well-structured organization of template files. Separation into subfolders, such as components, layouts and pages, facilitates code navigation and collaboration between teams. Each file has a clear responsibility, and standardized naming makes role identification intuitive. By organizing templates in this way, it becomes possible to scale the application without compromising readability or rendering performance.

Rendering security must also be considered, as injecting data from external sources can pose risks. Jinja2 automatically implements special character escaping to prevent cross-site scripting (XSS) attacks. However, when using the |safe filter to mark a string as safe, it is important to ensure that the data is already sanitized, avoiding vulnerabilities. The security policy must be clear and applied consistently across all templates that receive dynamic data.

Robust integration between Flask and Jinja2 allows the application to act as a unified platform for data presentation and user interaction. Separation of responsibilities and modularization of interface components reduce complexity and promote agile development. The flexibility of Jinja2, combined with the simplicity of Flask, makes it possible to create responsive, scalable and easy-to-maintain systems, adapted to the demands of contemporary projects.

When working with Jinja2, you can take advantage of several advanced features, such as creating custom filters that transform data in specific ways. For example, a filter can be created to format monetary values or dates according to the user's location. These filters are registered in the Flask app and automatically apply to the rendered data, improving the user experience without adding complexity to the template.

Rendering performance can be optimized using techniques such as template caching. By caching rendered HTML, the server can respond to subsequent requests more quickly, reducing processing time and easing the load on systems with high volume of access. This strategy is particularly useful in applications that present static content or that do not change frequently, allowing the user to receive the response with minimal latency.

The organization and modularization of templates, combined with the application of good development practices, ensure that the maintenance and evolution of the interface do not become bottlenecks in the project. Each component, from the base layout to individual components like menus and forms, is designed with a focus on reusability and simplicity. The combination of dynamic rendering, inheritance and component inclusion allows the development team to adapt the interface as new demands arise, without the need to rewrite large parts of the code.

The experience accumulated when using Jinja2 in real projects shows that the flexibility of this mechanism is capable of serving everything from small websites to complex corporate applications. The ease of integration with modern frameworks, the ability to handle complex data and the simplicity of writing templates make it an indispensable tool for anyone who wants to build dynamic web interfaces. Continuing to use good practices, such as the use of Blueprints to organize routes and the separation of template files into logical structures, contributes to sustainable, high-quality development.

For teams that work with multiple developers, standardizing templates facilitates versioning and collaboration. Version control tools, such as Git, integrated with Continuous Integration systems, allow changes to templates to be reviewed, tested and integrated securely, avoiding conflicts and regressions. The use of unit tests to verify the rendering of templates also contributes to the reliability of the system, ensuring that each change preserves the integrity of the presented interface.

Maintaining templates also involves constant adaptation to new demands, whether through the inclusion of new sections or the need for compatibility with different devices and browsers. The modularity of the components allows updates to a single file to be automatically propagated to all pages that depend on it, optimizing the development cycle and reducing the time required to implement design changes. Integration with modern CSS and JavaScript frameworks enhances this approach, enabling the creation of responsive and interactive interfaces.

Challenges encountered during template development can range from compatibility issues to performance issues. Rapid diagnosis and the application of troubleshooting techniques are essential to minimize impacts. Error messages provided by Flask in debug mode point to syntax errors or problems in template logic, allowing the team to correct any discrepancies without major delays. In-depth knowledge of Jinja2 resources, combined with well-structured internal documentation, facilitates problem solving and the transmission of knowledge between team members.

Digital transformation requires web applications to be not only functional, but also visually attractive and intuitive. Using Jinja2 in conjunction with Flask allows you to create interfaces that meet these requirements, combining server logic with sophisticated presentation. The clear separation between data and presentation ensures that design changes can be made without interfering with business logic, facilitating frequent updates and adaptation to new design trends.

The continuous evolution of web technologies requires developers to always be on the lookout for new features and best practices. Jinja2 has evolved alongside the Python ecosystem, adopting performance improvements and new features that expand its rendering capacity. The active community of developers contributes plugins, custom filters, and extensions that can be integrated into Flask, enriching the development environment and enabling innovative solutions to complex problems.

The practical and theoretical approach adopted by this manual provides an in-depth understanding of how Jinja2 works and its integration with Flask, demonstrating how each feature can be applied to build dynamic, scalable, high-quality web interfaces. The combination of code, template structuring and modularization techniques forms a robust set that serves as the basis for the development of modern applications, meeting the needs of a market in constant transformation.

Deepening knowledge in Jinja2 is an investment that allows developers to create systems with a more consistent interface that is easy to maintain and quickly adapts to changes. The clarity of the syntax, combined with the flexibility of the inheritance and inclusion mechanisms, makes building templates an intuitive and powerful task. Constant practice, analysis of real cases and the exploration of advanced resources ensure that professionals remain updated and able to face challenges in projects of any scale.

By mastering the fundamentals, organization and advanced rendering techniques with Jinja2, it is possible to transform the way data is presented to users, promoting a user experience that combines efficiency, aesthetics and functionality. This integration between backend and frontend, mediated by well-structured templates, establishes a standard of excellence that is reflected in robust and adaptable applications, capable of meeting the demands of a constantly evolving digital environment.

The path to excellence involves a detailed understanding of each tool and resource available, the practice of good development practices and the constant search for improvements. The ability to create templates that are both dynamic and organized allows applications to not only respond to current needs, but also prepare for future challenges, integrating new technologies and trends without compromising system stability and efficiency. By applying the concepts presented, any developer will be able to increase the quality of their applications' interface, ensuring that design and functionality work together in harmony.

Rendering with Jinja2 makes it possible to transform raw data into valuable, visually pleasing information, using a combination of logic and markup to create user experiences that stand out for their clarity and efficiency. The careful implementation of each resource, from the definition of blocks and macros to the organization of templates and components, contributes to the creation of a robust system, where each part fulfills a specific role and interacts coherently with the whole. In-depth knowledge of these resources is essential for anyone who wants to build modern and scalable web applications, capable of responding to a dynamic and competitive market.

Integrating the concepts covered in this guide with agile and collaborative development practices allows teams to develop high-quality solutions quickly and safely. The standardization of templates, the reuse of components and the adoption of automatic documentation tools form an ecosystem where communication between parties becomes natural and intuitive, minimizing errors and accelerating the development cycle. The experience gained when working with Jinja2 and Flask prepares professionals to face real challenges, transforming ideas into concrete and efficient applications.

The journey through Jinja2's features shows how separating logic and presentation can be the key to success in web development projects. By applying modularization, inheritance and inclusion techniques, it is possible to build interfaces that easily adapt to changes, promoting the consistency and scalability necessary to face future demands. Mastering these concepts enables developers to create applications that not only meet current needs, but also remain flexible and resilient in the face of constant evolution in the digital market.

Constant practice and exploration of new features, such as creating custom filters and macros, reinforce the importance of investing time in learning the ins and outs of Jinja2. Each improvement and each new technique learned contributes to a solid foundation that is reflected in the quality of the applications developed. This dedication ensures that professionals remain updated and ready to innovate, adapting best practices to the specific demands of their projects.

The smooth integration between Flask and Jinja2 represents one of the most powerful solutions for creating modern web applications. With the combination of a lightweight and flexible framework and a robust template engine, developers can focus on creating innovative features, without giving up clarity and organization in data presentation. The separation of responsibilities and modularization of components are fundamental to the success of any project, allowing each part to be updated and improved independently, without compromising the system as a whole.

By applying the knowledge acquired, it becomes possible to build dynamic and responsive interfaces that adapt to different contexts and devices, ensuring a consistent and pleasant user experience. The use of advanced rendering techniques, combined with a structured organization of templates, forms the basis for the development of solutions that stand out for their efficiency and elegance. This approach promotes the creation of applications that not only work robustly, but also delight users with their refined and intuitive presentation.

The constant evolution of web technologies requires professionals to constantly learn and adapt. Mastering Jinja2, combined with the efficient use of Flask, represents a significant competitive advantage for those who want to create scalable, high-performance applications. The ability to transform dynamic data into impactful visual interfaces is a differentiator that is reflected in successful products and a better experience for the end user.

By the end of this session, understanding the fundamentals of Jinja2, organizing and creating templates, inheritance and inclusion techniques, and practical rendering examples provide a robust foundation for developing modern web interfaces. This foundation allows developers to build applications with a clear separation between business logic and presentation, promoting maintenance, scalability and continuous evolution of projects.

The integration of the concepts presented here with daily practice in web development establishes a standard of excellence that prepares any professional to face the challenges of a market in constant transformation. Investment in knowledge and rigorous application of good practices result in systems that combine functionality, design and efficiency, transforming the user experience and raising the level of solutions developed.

Each component, each macro, each template block and each route that interacts with these files makes up a harmonious set that, when well executed, allows the creation of intuitive, consistent and robust interfaces. This modular, dynamic and reuse-oriented approach not only optimizes development time, but also guarantees the quality and maintenance of systems in the long term. With these fundamentals and practices, building dynamic and modern web applications becomes an accessible and enjoyable task, capable of transforming ideas into real solutions that positively impact the users' experience.

CHAPTER 8. WORKING WITH FORMS AND VALIDATION

Creating and processing forms is often a key point in many web applications, as users interact through fields and buttons that send data to the server. In a development flow with Flask, several features simplify the capture, validation and manipulation of this information. A coherent structure reduces security issues, improves usability and facilitates error diagnosis. By combining good code organization practices and appropriate extensions, the application becomes more reliable and enjoyable for those who use it.

A well-designed system typically features one or more forms that collect important data such as user registrations, contact submissions, login and profile updates. The way these fields are defined and validated impacts the quality of the stored data. The ability to validate that values are in an expected format, do not exceed size limits and satisfy uniqueness rules, for example, increases robustness. Errors in early stages can lead to vulnerabilities or inconsistencies that are reflected in future failures.

Flask offers native mechanisms to handle sending data via POST method. The developer accesses this information via request.form or request.files, depending on the field type. For more advanced needs, extensions like Flask-WTF bring a built-in validation suite, CSRF attack protection, and forms management. Combining these tools with design practices, such as displaying clear error and feedback messages, results in more intuitive interfaces.

Displaying failures when validating fields is essential. Without feedback on possible problems, the user feels lost and may abandon the process. Messages that indicate exactly which field is incorrect, and why, make filling it out simpler. The use of flash messages or inline display below the fields ensures the clarity of the flow. This interaction needs to be accompanied by security mechanisms to prevent improper manipulations or code injection attacks. The CSRF token, generated with each request, prevents external sites from forcing submissions on behalf of users, protecting the system.

The adoption of best practices for data capture includes checking mandatory fields, size limits, formatting standards (such as valid emails) and information coherence. If the user enters a number outside the accepted range, the system must report the failure. In some scenarios, validation involves complex rules that combine multiple fields or query the database to avoid duplicates. Organizing these checks in a modular, reusable way simplifies future expansion by making it easy to add new forms or change rules without redoing all the logic.

Form creation and processing

The most direct way to handle forms in Flask is to render an HTML file with fields and then write routes that process the POST data. The basic flow involves two steps: displaying the form when the request is GET and receiving the data when the request is POST. The following code snippet illustrates this dynamic without resorting to additional extensions:

python

```
# EXAMPLE 1
# STEP 1: imports
from flask import Flask, render_template, request, redirect, url_for

app = Flask(__name__)
```

```python
app.config["SECRET_KEY"] = "some_very_secret_key"

# PASSO 2: route to show the form
@app.route("/contact", methods=["GET"])
def contact_form():
    return render_template("contact_form.html")

# PASSO 3: route to process the form
@app.route("/contact", methods=["POST"])
def contact_process():
    name = request.form.get("name")
    email = request.form.get("email")
    message = request.form.get("message")

    if not name or not email:
        # Possibly redirect back with an error or handle the
problem
        return redirect(url_for("contact_form"))

    # Any additional logic, like saving to a database or sending
an email
    return f"Data received: {name}, {email}, {message}"

if __name__ == "__main__":
    app.run(debug=True)
```

The HTML file containing the form can be organized as follows:

html

```html
<!DOCTYPE html>
<html>
<head>
    <meta charset="utf-8">
    <title>Contact</title>
</head>
<body>
    <h1>Contact Form</h1>
```

```
<form method="POST"
action="{{ url_for('contact_process') }}">
    <label>Name:</label>
    <input type="text" name="name" required>

    <label>Email:</label>
    <input type="email" name="email" required>

    <label>Message:</label>
    <textarea name="message"></textarea>

    <button type="submit">Send</button>
  </form>
</body>
</html>
```

This project allows the user to access the /contact endpoint via GET to view the form and the same endpoint to be called via POST when clicking "Send." The contact_process route receives data via request.form, performs basic checks and returns text. In a real project, it would be worth including some clear error feedback if information is missing, but this example demonstrates the structure.

Common Errors and How to Fix Them:

1. Bad Request (400)
   The server was unable to process the request due to missing or invalid data.
   Probable cause: Form without required fields, or incorrect HTML that does not send data.
   Solution: Adjust the name of the inputs and ensure the presence of method="POST".
2. TypeError when accessing form values
   Occurs if the route expects something that does not exist in request.form.
   Probable cause: Lack of verification or field name

differing from what was defined in the HTML.
Solution: Use request.form.get("campo") and keep field names consistent.

Data validation with extensions (Flask-WTF)

For cases where more elaborate validations are required, Flask-WTF provides integration with WTForms and makes it easy to set up CSRF tokens. This extension creates a Python class for each form, concentrating validation rules in one place. If the user omits fields or enters non-standard values, the process is interrupted and error messages become available.

bash

```bash
pip install flask-wtf
```

A forms.py file can contain:

python

```python
# EXAMPLE 2
# STEP 1: import FlaskForm and needed fields
from flask_wtf import FlaskForm
from wtforms import StringField, TextAreaField, SubmitField
from wtforms.validators import DataRequired, Email, Length

class ContactForm(FlaskForm):
    name = StringField("Name", validators=[DataRequired(),
Length(min=2, max=50)])
    email = StringField("Email", validators=[DataRequired(),
Email()])
    message = TextAreaField("Message",
validators=[Length(max=500)])
    submit = SubmitField("Send")
```

The main Flask application imports this class, creating instances of the form that encapsulate the validations:

python

```python
# EXAMPLE 3
# ESTEP 1: main application using the form
from flask import Flask, render_template, redirect, url_for
from forms import ContactForm

app = Flask(__name__)
app.config["SECRET_KEY"] = "some_very_secret_key"

@app.route("/contact", methods=["GET", "POST"])
def contact():
    form = ContactForm()
    if form.validate_on_submit():
        name = form.name.data
        email = form.email.data
        message = form.message.data
        # Example logic: store data or send an email
        return redirect(url_for("success"))
    return render_template("contact_wtf.html", form=form)

@app.route("/success")
def success():
    return "Form submitted successfully!"

if __name__ == "__main__":
    app.run(debug=True)
```

The contact_wtf.html template includes form rendering and displays error messages:

html

```html
<!DOCTYPE html>
<html>
<head>
    <meta charset="utf-8">
    <title>Contact with Flask-WTF</title>
```

```html
</head>
<body>
  <h1>Contact Form</h1>
  <form method="POST">
    {{ form.hidden_tag() }}

    <div>
      {{ form.name.label }}<br>
      {{ form.name }}<br>
      {% for error in form.name.errors %}
        <span style="color: red;">{{ error }}</span><br>
      {% endfor %}
    </div>

    <div>
      {{ form.email.label }}<br>
      {{ form.email }}<br>
      {% for error in form.email.errors %}
        <span style="color: red;">{{ error }}</span><br>
      {% endfor %}
    </div>

    <div>
      {{ form.message.label }}<br>
      {{ form.message }}<br>
      {% for error in form.message.errors %}
        <span style="color: red;">{{ error }}</span><br>
      {% endfor %}
    </div>

    {{ form.submit }}
  </form>
</body>
</html>
```

The validate_on_submit() function checks whether the

request is POST and whether all validators have been satisfied. If any field fails, the template displays individual errors next to the inputs. hidden_tag() holds the CSRF token and other metadata. It is essential that app.config["SECRET_KEY"] is set for token protection to work.

Common Errors and How to Fix Them:

1. CSRF token missing
   Indicates that the form does not contain the expected token.
   Probable cause: Missing form.hidden_tag() or undefined SECRET_KEY.
   Solution: Make sure form.hidden_tag() is in the HTML and SECRET_KEY is configured.
2. Error messages not displayed
   The if form.validate_on_submit() fails, but the user does not see messages.
   Probable cause: Missing {% for error in form.field.errors %} loop or inconsistent field names.
   Solution: Check each field in the template, using the same name defined in forms.py.
3. The form always returns false in validate_on_submit()
   Something prevents successful validation even when the fields are correct.
   Probable cause: Divergent fields, method different from POST or token problems.
   Solution: Review method="POST," the inclusion of the token and whether the keys in the HTML match those in forms.py.

Displaying error messages and feedback

Good applications clearly signal what happened after a form submission. Errors must be displayed so that the user knows what to correct. Success messages reinforce that the operation was successful. Flask offers a flash function to store messages that persist until the next request, allowing the use of a more global feedback pattern.

python

```python
# EXAMPLE 4
# STEP 1: example with flash messages
from flask import Flask, render_template, redirect, url_for, flash
from forms import ContactForm

app = Flask(__name__)
app.config["SECRET_KEY"] = "another_secret_key"

@app.route("/contact", methods=["GET", "POST"])
def contact():
    form = ContactForm()
    if form.validate_on_submit():
        flash("Form submitted successfully!")
        return redirect(url_for("contact"))
    return render_template("contact_flash.html", form=form)

if __name__ == "__main__":
    app.run(debug=True)
```

The contact_flash.html template can display these messages using get_flashed_messages():

html

```html
<!DOCTYPE html>
<html>
<head>
    <meta charset="utf-8">
    <title>Contact with Flash</title>
</head>
<body>
    {% with messages = get_flashed_messages() %}
```

```
    {% if messages %}
       <ul>
       {% for msg in messages %}
          <li style="color: green;">{{ msg }}</li>
       {% endfor %}
       </ul>
    {% endif %}
  {% endwith %}

  <form method="POST">
     {{ form.hidden_tag() }}

     <label>{{ form.name.label }}</label><br>
     {{ form.name }}<br>
     {% for error in form.name.errors %}
        <span style="color: red;">{{ error }}</span><br>
     {% endfor %}

     <label>{{ form.email.label }}</label><br>
     {{ form.email }}<br>
     {% for error in form.email.errors %}
        <span style="color: red;">{{ error }}</span><br>
     {% endfor %}

     <label>{{ form.message.label }}</label><br>
     {{ form.message }}<br>
     {% for error in form.message.errors %}
        <span style="color: red;">{{ error }}</span><br>
     {% endfor %}

     {{ form.submit }}
  </form>
</body>
</html>
```

When the user fills in everything correctly, the application executes form.validate_on_submit() and calls flash("Form submitted successfully!"), returning a redirect. On subsequent GET, the message is displayed in green. If something is missing, specific errors appear below each field.

Common Errors and How to Fix Them:

1. Duplicate messages
   The user sees the same message every time they reload the page.
   Probable cause: Lack of redirect or unconditional flash repetition.
   Solution: Use redirect after flash, ensuring that the message is displayed only once.
2. Message does not appear
   get_flashed_messages() returns empty, even though there is flash.
   Probable cause: Lack of flash import or flash execution occurred after redirect, making storage impossible.
   Solution: Check the order, import and mode of use of the flash function.

Best practices for data capture

Data capture requires care that encompasses design, validation and security. Some relevant points:

1. Use of CSRF Token
   Prevent external applications from forcing submissions. The token generated by Flask-WTF prevents Cross-Site Request Forgery attacks.
2. Suitable validators
   Each field has its own characteristics. Emails require Email(), required fields require DataRequired(), text limits use Length(), and so on. Custom validators help with specific rules, such as checking if a user already exists in the database.
3. Clear error messages

Indicate exactly the field that failed and suggest corrections. Generic errors disorient the user and reduce the effectiveness of the form.

4. User-friendly layout
   Organize fields so that it is easy to understand the filling sequence. Use styles that highlight flaws in an intuitive way.

5. Modular code structure
   Declaring forms in separate classes avoids confusion and facilitates unit testing and maintenance.

6. Database integration
   After validating and sanitizing the data, store it correctly using parameterized queries or ORMs, protecting against injections.

7. Maintain coherence and security
   Do not record passwords in plain text. Apply hashing and salting. Delete sensitive data when unnecessary.

8. Collaborative front-end
   Javascript can validate some of the fields to provide immediate feedback, but server-side validation remains critical.

9. Automated Tests
   Check form filling flows. Ensure that failure scenarios are handled and that error messages appear.

10. Observation of logs and alerts
    When something fails, debug logs can show tracebacks indicating where and why the exception arose. Error messages should help identify incorrect or missing fields.

Troubleshooting and Code Formatting Rules

Maintaining the pattern of placing code snippets in blocks, with comments like # STEP 1 and # EXAMPLE 1, makes it easier to read. Identifying each part of the script makes learning more didactic, as the reader understands the logical sequence.

Creating a Common Errors and How to Fix Them section helps code entry solve problems.

Using coherent indentation and self-explanatory variables improves clarity. Tools like black and isort standardize formatting, while flake8 identifies inconsistencies. In large projects, dividing the logic of forms, routes, and data models helps reduce complexity. Each file maintains focus on one responsibility, simplifying maintenance.

Interaction with forms is part of everyday life in any web system that needs to collect data. It's not just about displaying fields, but about processing values, checking coherence, providing feedback and ensuring security against malicious actions or out-of-scope input. The adoption of Flask-WTF and its validations simplifies much of this flow, allowing the developer to focus on business rules instead of repetitively writing the same checks. The presentation of errors in detail guides the user in correcting fields, improving the experience.

The quality of form handling has a direct impact on the reliability of the database, as invalid entries can generate inconsistencies that are difficult to repair. Integration with CSRF tokens reduces threats, and code modularization facilitates future evolutions. A team that masters these practices builds robust applications, where each form follows similar validation, feedback, and design standards. This results in consistency, simple maintenance and less propensity for bugs.

Over time, new fields, routes or specific validations may be added. Keeping everything documented and organized avoids rework. Systematic use of databases with ORMs or well-planned queries ensures that accepted data is recorded correctly. Security awareness ensures that tokens, passwords and sensitive data are treated rigorously. In short, formulating a solid foundation for processing user input defines the quality level of the entire application, as this stage is where the external world interacts and shapes the internal logic of the system.

CHAPTER 9. INTEGRATION WITH DATABASES IN FLASK

The development of robust web applications in Flask often requires data persistence in a database, whether to store information about users, products, posts or any type of relevant entity. Adopting an ORM (Object-Relational Mapping) facilitates this interaction by creating a bridge between Python data structures and relational database tables. SQLAlchemy stands out as one of the most used libraries for this purpose, as it combines performance, flexibility and good architectural practices.

A coherent implementation takes care of the entire journey, from the initial database configuration, through table and object modeling, to CRUD (Create, Read, Update, Delete) operations. The ability to version schemas and apply incremental migrations ensures that structure changes occur in a controlled manner, avoiding information losses or inconsistencies. The flow becomes even more organized when the model definitions are separated into specific files, following modularity principles that simplify maintenance in medium to large projects.

The introduction to SQLAlchemy begins with the distinction between its Core and its ORM. Core offers direct access to SQL expressions and is useful in situations where greater control over queries is desired. ORM allows you to map Python classes to tables, facilitating the manipulation of records as objects. This style of abstraction reduces the amount of manual SQL code and harmonizes data persistence with the application language.

Configuring connections to databases, such as PostgreSQL, MySQL, SQLite and other systems, requires defining connection strings and creating an instance of the SQLAlchemy engine. In Flask, the Flask-SQLAlchemy library further simplifies this process by providing native integration with the framework environment. This extension eliminates some of the repetitive configuration, but still allows access to the full power of SQLAlchemy.

Data modeling and CRUD operations are at the heart of any application that manipulates persistent information. Each entity becomes a Python class with attributes that represent columns of a table, while additional methods can encapsulate specific logic. Insert, query, update, and remove operations are performed by invoking methods from the ORM, which generates SQL under the hood. This method centralizes business rules in Python classes and methods, avoiding the proliferation of SQL statements scattered throughout the application.

Finally, migrations and schema versioning generate a history of changes to the database. Each update to the table structure (addition of columns, indexes, foreign keys) is recorded as a migration script that can be applied or rolled back. The Alembic tool stands out for this purpose and, when integrated with Flask, facilitates the evolution of the schema in an incremental and safe way.

Introduction to SQLAlchemy and ORM

SQLAlchemy is a mature and widely adopted project in the Python ecosystem. It allows you to interact with relational databases through queries expressed in Python, instead of raw SQL strings. The SQLAlchemy ORM defines mappings between classes and tables, transforming each instance into a database record. This style boosts productivity, as operations such as creating a user or updating information are reduced to attribute manipulations and ORM session invocations.

Some benefits:

1. Reduced repetitive SQL code.
2. Greater clarity in the organization of queries and models.
3. Caching and lazy loading mechanisms to optimize access.
4. Robust relationship handling (one-to-many, many-to-many, etc.).
5. Integration with migration tools and support for multiple banks.

Adopting SQLAlchemy does not prevent the use of direct SQL queries when necessary. Specific situations may require advanced optimizations or custom instructions. Still, most scenarios benefit from the ORM style, which keeps the application clean and easy to understand.

Configuring database connections

One of the first steps is to define how the application will connect to the bank. The Flask-SQLAlchemy library adds a layer that handles integration and simplifies the creation of sessions to interact with the database. To install:

bash

```
pip install flask-sqlalchemy
```

In a main file, such as app.py, you can establish the configuration:

python

```
# EXAMPLE 1
# STEP 1: imports
from flask import Flask
from flask_sqlalchemy import SQLAlchemy
```

```
app = Flask(__name__)
# PASSO 2: config string for database connection
app.config["SQLALCHEMY_DATABASE_URI"] = "sqlite:///
mydatabase.db"
app.config["SQLALCHEMY_TRACK_MODIFICATIONS"] = False

# PASSO 3: instantiating the db object
db = SQLAlchemy(app)

if __name__ == "__main__":
    app.run(debug=True)
```

In this example, the application uses a local SQLite file called mydatabase.db. In larger projects, it would be common to use a robust DBMS like PostgreSQL, replacing the connection string with something like postgresql+psycopg2://username:password@localhost/mydatabase.

Common Errors and How to Fix Them:

1. ModuleNotFoundError: No module named 'psycopg2'
   Occurs if the application configures PostgreSQL without installing the psycopg2 dependency.
   Probable cause: Failure to install the driver.
   Solution: Run pip install psycopg2-binary or pip install psycopg2 depending on the environment.

2. sqlalchemy.exc.OperationalError
   Appears when the connection string is incorrect or the bank is not accessible.
   Probable cause: Invalid username, password or host, or inoperative bank server.
   Solution: Check if the bank address, credentials and port are correct.

3. RuntimeError: application not registered on db instance and no application bound to current

context
Indicates problem with Flask context when starting SQLAlchemy.
Probable cause: Incorrect use of the application and db object creation pattern.
Solution: Link app to db or use the factory pattern, calling init_app(app) if adopted.

Data modeling and CRUD operations

Defining a model is the step that transforms a Python class into a database table. Each attribute corresponds to a column and can have types such as String, Integer, Boolean, DateTime, among others. It is possible to add specific constraints, relationships and configurations.

python

```python
# EXAMPLE 2
# PASSO 1: importing the db instance
from app import db

class User(db.Model):
    # PASSO 2: table name and columns
    __tablename__ = "users"

    id = db.Column(db.Integer, primary_key=True)
    username = db.Column(db.String(50), unique=True,
nullable=False)
    email = db.Column(db.String(120), unique=True,
nullable=False)
    active = db.Column(db.Boolean, default=True)

    # PASSO 3: a custom method for demonstration
    def __repr__(self):
        return f"<User {self.username}>"
```

The @property decorator and additional methods can enrich

the class with specific logic. Once defined, the application can create the corresponding table by calling db.create_all() or using migrations.

CRUD operations become simple when using SQLAlchemy Session, encapsulated by db.session in Flask-SQLAlchemy:

python

```
# EXAMPLE 3
# STEP 1: creating a new user
new_user = User(username="alice",
email="alice@example.com")

# STEP 2: adding to the session
db.session.add(new_user)

# STEP 3: committing to persist in the database
db.session.commit()
```

To query records, the class defines methods such as query.filter_by(...).first() or query.all():

python

```
# EXAMPLE 4
# STEP 1: retrieving all active users
active_users = User.query.filter_by(active=True).all()
for user in active_users:
    print(user.username, user.email)
```

To update, simply modify attributes and commit:

python

```
# EXAMPLE 5
# STEP 1: retrieving a user
user = User.query.filter_by(username="alice").first()
# STEP 2: updating fields
```

```
user.email = "alice.new@example.com"
# STEP 3: committing the changes
db.session.commit()
```

To delete:

python

```
# EXAMPLE 6
user_to_delete = User.query.get(1)
if user_to_delete:
    db.session.delete(user_to_delete)
    db.session.commit()
```

Common Errors and How to Fix Them:

1. sqlalchemy.exc.IntegrityError
   It usually occurs if the table requires unique or non-null values and the application tries to insert conflicting data.
   Probable cause: Trying to insert a duplicate email into a unique column, for example.
   Solution: Check uniqueness before insertion, catch the exception or remove the constraint depending on the business rule.
2. AttributeError: 'NoneType' object has no attribute '...'
   Appears when the query does not find any records and returns None.
   Probable cause: Lack of checking whether user_to_delete exists.
   Solution: Include an if user_to_delete: before accessing the object.
3. sqlalchemy.orm.exc.DetachedInstanceError
   Appears if an object has been removed from the session and is being manipulated again without association.
   Probable cause: Early termination of the session or

manipulation in another context.

Solution: Access the attributes before closing the session or reattaching the object.

Schema migrations and versioning

In projects that evolve, it is common to need to change the database structure: add columns, change types, create new tables. Alembic is SQLAlchemy's default tool for migrations, and the Flask-Migrate extension integrates Alembic with Flask in a simple way. Installation:

bash

```
pip install flask-migrate
```

In the main file, you can configure Flask-Migrate:

python

```
# EXAMPLE 7
# STEP 1: imports
from flask import Flask
from flask_sqlalchemy import SQLAlchemy
from flask_migrate import Migrate

app = Flask(__name__)
app.config["SQLALCHEMY_DATABASE_URI"] = "sqlite:///
mydatabase.db"
app.config["SQLALCHEMY_TRACK_MODIFICATIONS"] = False

db = SQLAlchemy(app)
migrate = Migrate(app, db)

if __name__ == "__main__":
    app.run(debug=True)
```

In the terminal, some operations are available:

bash

```
flask db init
flask db migrate -m "Initial migration."
flask db upgrade
```

Each migration generates a script in the migrations/ directory, containing instructions for creating, altering, or removing tables and columns. The upgrade command applies the change, and downgrade reverts it. This way, the team maintains a versioned record of the schema, avoiding surprises when deploying to production.

Example of a generated migration script (partially edited for demonstration):

python

```python
# EXAMPLE 8
# STEP 1: auto-generated by Alembic
def upgrade():
    op.create_table(
        "users",
        sa.Column("id", sa.Integer(), nullable=False),
        sa.Column("username", sa.String(length=50), nullable=False),
        sa.Column("email", sa.String(length=120), nullable=False),
        sa.Column("active", sa.Boolean(), nullable=True),
        sa.PrimaryKeyConstraint("id"),
        sa.UniqueConstraint("email"),
        sa.UniqueConstraint("username")
    )

def downgrade():
    op.drop_table("users")
```

Alembic analyzes the current model and compares it with the bank's structure, creating appropriate instructions. You can manually edit these scripts to refine the logic if you need to manipulate data during the transition.

Common Errors and How to Fix Them:

1. sqlalchemy.exc.OperationalError during migration
   Occurs if the migration attempts to create or change something that conflicts with existing constraints.
   Probable cause: Columns with duplicate constraints, or columns already existing in the schema.
   Solution: Adjust the migration script to handle old data or remove unnecessary constraints.

2. AttributeError: module 'migrations' has no attribute '...'
   It may appear when the project has not initialized correctly or the environment variables are not defined.
   Probable cause: Flask db init failed to run or the folder structure is non-standard.
   Solution: Perform init and keep the migrations/ directory in the same location as the manage script.

3. Targets Not Up to Date
   It happens when the model structure in the code is different from what Alembic recognizes as updated.
   Probable cause: Failed to run flask db upgrade before running flask db migrate again.
   Solution: Apply pending migrations or revert to the previous state, synchronizing model and schema.

Troubleshooting and Code Formatting Rules

Following a code segmentation strategy, adding # EXAMPLE X and # STEP Y, makes the text didactic. Adding a "Common Errors and How to Fix Them" section helps with quick diagnosis. Each script must be functional and maintain proper indentation.

Identifying each part of the script, such as imports, configuration, template creation, and execution, helps both those reading and typing the code. Avoid very extensive codes in a single block, preferring to divide them into short steps. In large applications, separating models.py, config.py, and migrations/ (by Alembic) ensures that each file fulfills a specific function and facilitates long-term maintenance.

When adding relationships (one-to-many, many-to-many) and advanced settings, the same organization and troubleshooting principle applies. In the case of failures, the SQLAlchemy message usually contains details about the query generated and the error returned by the database. Logging this message and comparing it with the model logic is the way to solve problems.

Most errors arise from discrepancies between what is defined in the model and what already exists in the bank. Keeping the migration base clean and applying changes incrementally avoids confusion. The development team must always update its local databases before introducing new changes, reducing conflicts.

The adoption of an ORM such as SQLAlchemy, combined with Flask's functionalities, enables agile and sustainable development. The code gains expressiveness by manipulating records as Python objects, without writing repetitive SQL. The Flask-SQLAlchemy extension minimizes redundant configuration and provides simplified session access, while Flask-Migrate and Alembic securely manage schema evolution.

From a design point of view, each entity defines a class that mirrors the table in the database. This arrangement promotes clarity because the entire application shares a unified data model. The orchestration of complex relationships, such as posts that belong to users or orders that contain multiple products, becomes more predictable thanks to the cardinality and foreign key features defined in the ORM.

Using migrations ensures that the evolution of tables is tracked, allowing different team members to synchronize changes without overwriting existing data. This control is invaluable in systems that require stability and traceability.

CRUD operations are simpler and less prone to error, as database manipulation is mediated by the ORM layer. Creating new records involves instantiating a class and making commits, updating is just assigning new values to attributes, and deleting is removing the object from the session. Queries use the query interface, transforming queries into Python expressions rather than manual SQL statements.

However, flexibility remains: highly specific or demanding queries can rely on SQLAlchemy Core or even raw SQL statements if advanced optimization is required. This balance between abstraction and low-level access suits both those who prefer the convenience of ORM and those who need custom configurations.

Maintaining good project organization practices, with separate modules for configurations, models and routes, strengthens code cohesion. The adoption of logs and the implementation of automated tests aimed at bank access detect regressions at early stages. The application of patterns such as Repository or Service Layer can increase robustness, further isolating the persistence and business logic layers.

In summary, database integration in Flask, through SQLAlchemy and its ecosystem, lays a solid foundation for dynamic applications that manage persistent data. A well-designed configuration, combined with schema versioning, ensures security and consistency throughout the project life cycle. Standardization in the use of CRUD, clarity in modeling and care with relationships provide the basis for scalable and organized systems, ready to deal with medium and large scenarios without sacrificing quality or development speed.

CHAPTER 10. AUTHENTICATION AND AUTHORIZATION IN FLASK

Creating applications that require restricted access or profile management involves setting up a secure process for identifying and controlling permissions. Flask allows you to implement login, logout and session handling flows in an integrated way, supported by extensions that simplify the administration of sensitive data. This mechanism ensures that only authorized people enter critical areas, also defining which resources each group can view or change. Sessions are blocks of data that reside on the server or in signed cookies, allowing the system to recognize the user on each request without the need to authenticate repeatedly. Flask-Login appears as one of the most popular add-ons, as it manages all the logic of remembering whether someone is logged in and ensuring that each route is blocked or released according to the credentials provided.

Authentication consists of proving someone's identity, whether by login and password, tokens, OAuth or other methods, while authorization decides whether that user can access or manipulate a certain resource. These concepts, although complementary, play different roles. The first step is always to confirm who is connecting, and then check if there are specific privileges. Modern applications often combine several techniques, including session cookies for web environments and JWT tokens in APIs. Flask allows you to customize this approach, but adopting consolidated standards saves rework and paves the way for future updates.

User sessions can be stored using signed cookies, where

the server attaches encrypted or secret-signed data and returns it to the browser. With each subsequent request, the browser sends this cookie, allowing Flask to retrieve the necessary information. Another alternative is to maintain the state on the server, uniquely identifying the user through an ID contained in the cookie. In both cases, an app.config["SECRET_KEY"] is essential to prevent fraud, as without this key an attacker could forge cookies. This value needs to be strong and well guarded, as his commitment leads to total control of the sessions.

The Flask-Login extension takes care of the fundamental flow of logging in, logging out, and checking permissions on specific routes. This feature set includes session management, login reminders, and protections against unauthenticated access. Usage begins with installation and import, defining a LoginManager object that links to Flask. This object is responsible for intercepting requests to protected routes, ensuring that only properly logged in users access them. This process preserves simplicity as each sensitive route can be decorated with a login_required, forcing authentication verification before proceeding.

The excerpt below shows how to configure Flask-Login in the environment:

python

```
# EXAMPLE 1
# STEP 1: imports and initialization
from flask import Flask, render_template, request, redirect,
url_for
from flask_sqlalchemy import SQLAlchemy
from flask_login import LoginManager, UserMixin, login_user,
logout_user, login_required, current_user

app = Flask(__name__)
app.config["SECRET_KEY"] = "any_very_secure_key"
```

```
app.config["SQLALCHEMY_DATABASE_URI"] = "sqlite:///
users.db"
app.config["SQLALCHEMY_TRACK_MODIFICATIONS"] = False

db = SQLAlchemy(app)

login_manager = LoginManager()
login_manager.init_app(app)
login_manager.login_view = "login"  # name of the login route
```

This login_manager manages the logic of redirecting logged out users to the login endpoint and storing the session after validation. The login_view defines where the user should go when trying to access a protected route without being authenticated. The UserMixin class makes it easy to integrate any model with Flask-Login by providing standard methods and properties such as is_authenticated or is_active.

Below is a user model integrated with SQLAlchemy, combining relevant columns and UserMixin inheritance:

python

```
# EXAMPLE 2
# STEP 1: user model
class User(db.Model, UserMixin):
    __tablename__ = "users"
    id = db.Column(db.Integer, primary_key=True)
    username = db.Column(db.String(64), unique=True,
nullable=False)
    password_hash = db.Column(db.String(128),
nullable=False)
    role = db.Column(db.String(32), default="user")

    def __repr__(self):
        return f"<User {self.username}>"
```

The role can be used to distinguish privileges, while password_hash stores the password in encrypted form (never in plain text). In the registration flow, you may want to apply secure hashing (e.g. bcrypt or scrypt). Flask-Login also requires a callback function that locates the user based on an ID stored in the session. This callback appears as user_loader:

python

```
# EXAMPLE 3
@login_manager.user_loader
def load_user(user_id):
    return User.query.get(int(user_id))
```

When the session indicates that a certain user is logged in, Flask-Login calls load_user, providing the ID to search for the corresponding object in the database. If not found, authentication will be invalidated.

To log in, you can create a route that validates your credentials. Once confirmed, login_user records success and generates the appropriate session:

python

```
# EXAMPLE 4
# STEP 1: login route
@app.route("/login", methods=["GET", "POST"])
def login():
    if request.method == "POST":
        username = request.form["username"]
        password = request.form["password"] # plain password
from form
        user = User.query.filter_by(username=username).first()
        if user and check_password(password,
user.password_hash):
```

```
        login_user(user)
        return redirect(url_for("protected"))
    return "Invalid credentials"
  return render_template("login.html")
```

check_password would be a function that compares the clear text password to the stored hash, using bcrypt or equivalent. The GET route displays a template with username and password fields, while the POST method handles the verification. login_user creates the session and marks this user as authenticated. The redirect can go to a successful route or the originally requested page.

Controlling permissions and access requires identifying who is logged in, which Flask-Login does through current_user. This object reflects the model instance, so using current_user.role or current_user.id retrieves persisted data. Sensitive routes can be decorated with login_required, ensuring that only authenticated people reach them:

python

```
# EXAMPLE 5
@app.route("/protected")
@login_required
def protected():
    return f"Hello, {current_user.username}. This is a protected
page."
```

If someone logged out tries to access, Flask-Login redirects to the configured login_view. This resolves the basic authentication flow, but does not yet differentiate permissions. To grant selective access, you can check the role before displaying content:

python

```python
# EXAMPLE 6
@app.route("/admin")
@login_required
def admin_area():
    if current_user.role != "admin":
        return "Access denied"
    return "Welcome to the admin area."
```

Checking the role field is a simple approach. In larger applications, you can create a system of groups and permissions, or integrate with an external identity server. Regardless of the scheme, Flask-Login remains responsible only for monitoring whether someone is logged in, delegating the access level logic to another module or to customizations in the model.

Logging out of the system involves releasing the session token and marking the user as unauthenticated:

python

```python
# EXAMPLE 7
@app.route("/logout")
@login_required
def logout():
    logout_user()
    return redirect(url_for("login"))
```

logout_user eliminates the information that links the current user to the bank ID from the session. The login_required in logout prevents any action if there is no user logged in, although in this case it doesn't make much difference.

To prevent session hijacking attacks, you may want to use HTTPS and set the cookie to secure, preventing it from being sent over unencrypted connections. The adoption of renewal tokens or rotating session IDs makes it difficult for an attacker

STUDIOD21 SMART TECH CONTENT

to use intercepted cookies. Adjusting expiration and inactivity times also improves protection, ending sessions that are inactive for a long time.

Data protection involves, in addition to the safe keeping of the SECRET_KEY, the adequate storage of passwords. It is essential to use key derivation functions such as bcrypt, argon2 or scrypt, which insert salt and repeat the hash. With this procedure, even if the bank is compromised, the passwords will not be exposed in plain text. Depending on your needs, you can implement password strength checking or extra questions to retrieve credentials.

In projects that require more sophisticated strategies, Flask can interoperate with OAuth 2.0 or SAML to authenticate via external services such as Google, GitHub or enterprise providers. In this flow, the application redirects the user to the provider, which validates the credentials and returns a token. Flask then records this token and extracts the profile information to build or update the local user. This method simplifies the process for users who already have accounts on known platforms, eliminating the need to create new passwords.

Access control, on the other hand, can be refined by using ACL or RBAC libraries. The idea is to model sets of permissions that apply to certain roles or even individually to each user. A route that handles confidential reports might check whether the user has the "view_reports" permission, while another that deletes records checks "delete_records." This level of granularity depends on the system design. In some cases, it is enough to divide the profile into admin and user, but in others, there are dozens of permissions to deal with.

Handling cookies with session tokens needs a well-defined lifecycle. The application can configure the cookie's expiration time, informing whether the session expires when closing the browser or whether it remains for a certain period of time.

Once the person closes the tab or is inactive for a long period of time, an idle timeout can invalidate the session on the server. This mechanism requires Flask or the associated layer to store the time of the user's last activity, perform the comparison with each request and terminate the session if it exceeds the limit.

When seeking high security, it is important to record login and logout events, or even failure attempts. This record may include IP, date and time, user agent and other information that facilitates auditing or detection of improper access. Connecting Flask logs to security analysis or monitoring systems helps detect anomalies, such as multiple failed attempts in a row or access from unusual locations.

In applications that deal with medical, financial or personal data, encrypting part of the content in the bank may be necessary, complementing the authentication part. In such scenarios, login ensures that only authorized users log in, but the server itself needs to handle encrypted data. In this case, key management and privilege segmentation solutions emerge, as even bank developers may be unable to read certain columns if they do not have the keys.

To simplify the development flow, some adopt scaffolding that generates ready-made login and logout routes, storing hashed passwords and providing authentication templates. This method speeds up prototypes and ensures a certain standardization, but those who want total control usually manually implement the login, logout and password recovery routes, following the practices mentioned. Unit and integration testing is crucial to confirm that restrictions work, as an oversight can open security holes or prevent legitimate users from accessing necessary areas.

When dealing with more complex permissions, it is possible to create a custom decorator that, in addition to login_required, checks whether the user meets additional requirements.

Something like:

python

```
def role_required(role_name):
    def decorator(func):
        @login_required
        def wrapper(*args, **kwargs):
            if current_user.role != role_name:
                return "Access denied"
            return func(*args, **kwargs)
        return wrapper
    return decorator

@app.route("/settings")
@role_required("admin")
def settings():
    return "Admin Settings"
```

This wrapper first requires authentication and then checks whether the role attribute matches the expected value, blocking if not. This can be expanded to accept multiple roles or even receive a whitelist. Because each application has unique requirements, the flexibility of Flask-Login and Flask allows logic to be fitted where it is most convenient.

It is important to plan the session token lifecycle, especially when managing logins across multiple devices or when the user changes passwords. In maximum security situations, forcing logout of all devices after a critical credential change prevents misuse of old tokens. This type of control requires the server to maintain a list of active sessions, associating each one with an ID and validating this record in the database before accepting the cookie session. If revoked, the session is invalidated on the basis, and a previously valid cookie will be rejected.

Data protection strategies also include monitoring whether

stored passwords meet certain complexity requirements. It is recommended to offer immediate feedback to the user, showing whether the password meets minimum standards, such as length and character diversity. However, the server must not store the actual password or display it in logs. In reset flows, sending temporary links or tokens via email, with an expiration date, replaces old practices that displayed passwords in the clear.

In terms of implementation, every route that handles sensitive data must use HTTPS to avoid interception of information, and headers such as Strict-Transport-Security can strengthen TLS enforcement. The session cookie must have the Secure and HttpOnly flags, blocking access via JavaScript and preventing sending over insecure connections. Large sessions or environments with multiple machines may require a shared repository for the sessions, such as Redis or a central database, ensuring that information is available regardless of which server receives the request.

When an application expands to a microservices ecosystem, distributed authentication becomes more complex, often relying on JWT or OAuth2 tokens. Flask adapts to these scenarios, but it is critical to synchronize expiration and revocation policies across all services. Each microservice must know how to validate tokens and how to find out if they have been revoked or expired. This level of complexity requires a more advanced approach, possibly integrating a centralized identity provider or an API gateway that coordinates authentication.

User authenticity is not limited to mere credentials. Some applications invest in additional factors, such as MFA (Multi-Factor Authentication), requesting a code sent by SMS or generated by a TOTP application. Flask accepts libraries that handle TOTP, integrating the login route with this extra factor if the user has MFA enabled. This type of increment drastically reduces the chance of hacking when someone obtains the password, but not the second factor.

It is also worth considering attempt limitation mechanisms, preventing brute force attacks. This practice implements counters on the server or bank, temporarily blocking the IP or account after several failed attempts. The blocking time increases progressively if insisted, discouraging automated attempts to discover passwords. In any of these processes, it is valuable to provide clear messages to the user, avoiding confusion and without revealing excessive details that make life easier for potential attackers.

The integration of each aspect — login, logout, session control, permissions checking, password hashing, cookie security, logs and auditing — generates a cohesive and attack-resistant ecosystem. Flask, due to its minimalist nature, does not require you to follow any specific standard, but provides hooks and extensions to make it flexible. Flask-Login does the authentication part well and provides a strong foundation for what comes next, which is establishing sophisticated authorization layers or exchanging session data with external services.

To maintain clear code maintenance, many prefer to separate the authentication flow into its own blueprint, containing the login, logout and password recovery routes. This blueprint registers with the main application and exports the Flask-Login callback functions. The user model can reside in another file, defining the columns and validation logic. This modular distribution simplifies team collaboration and reusing parts of the code in other projects.

It is also relevant to have tests that cover the login and logout flow. An integration test could simulate sending a POST with valid credentials and verify that the route redirects correctly. With invalid credentials, the failure message should be returned. When trying to access a protected route without authentication, the system must redirect to login. This procedure ensures that a future change does not break the authentication flow, especially when changing the way of storing sessions or implementing token logic.

In large-scale environments, sessions can overload the database if they are stored there. One option is to use distributed caches, such as Redis, to manage session state, avoiding intensive disk writes and reads. This approach improves performance, as session data recovery becomes faster and more scalable, especially if there are multiple Flask server replicas behind a load balancer. Each Flask instance needs to share access to the same session location.

Finally, the design of screens and templates that collect username and password must take care of usability details, such as clear error messages, support for reminding me to maintain the session beyond the default time, and warnings about downtime. When the user is redirected, it is good to remember which sensitive route they were trying to access, taking them there after successfully logging in. The adoption of flash messages guides the experience, showing whether the action was performed, whether the password was changed or whether permission was missing to view a certain resource.

In summary, Flask's login and session management application forms the basis of any system that separates the general public from protected areas. Using solid extensions like Flask-Login reduces the complexity of managing cookies, tokens, and callbacks, leading to reliable flows that ensure security. Access control and permissions can be built in layers, from simple profile checks to robust infrastructures with groups, roles, and privilege inheritance. Data protection involves a set of measures, such as password hashing, TLS for traffic, HttpOnly and Secure cookies, as well as logs that support auditing and monitoring. This set adjusts to the specific needs of each project, shaping authentication and authorization to provide simplicity for the end user, robustness for data and peace of mind for the developers who keep the system alive.

CHAPTER 11. COMMON FLASK ERRORS AND TROUBLESHOOTING

Flask applications can exhibit unexpected behavior in development or production environments, and pinpointing the source of a problem requires a systematic investigation strategy. Configuration failures, logical errors in routing, version conflicts between extensions and performance deficiencies are frequent occurrences, especially in projects that grow without rigorous organization. The diagnostic process includes monitoring logs, using debugging tools and carefully analyzing the flow of requests and dependencies. These techniques help to identify the exact cause of each inconvenience, making it possible to resolve or work around situations without compromising overall stability.

The first step is usually to understand when the failure appears. Some problems arise when starting the application, such as an exception when loading modules or a missing environment variable. Others only appear during specific requests, when a route has not been defined properly or an object is not available. In certain cases, the application works locally but fails on the production server, revealing environment divergences or unmet requirements. Observing the initial symptoms guides the search for the cause.

Common situations include import exceptions, such as ModuleNotFoundError, which occurs when Flask does not find the declared file or library. This failure indicates that the library was not installed or the name is spelled differently in the script. Checking the requirements.txt or pipenv/poetry file and ensuring that the package actually appears there is the first step. It is also useful to check whether the version of Python used locally matches that of the production environment, as differences can lead to different behaviors.

Some errors appear when starting the server: "Address already in use" appears when another application already occupies the port that Flask is trying to listen to. To work around it, you can end the process that is using the port or modify the Flask port using app.run(port=5001). If the message is "ValueError: signal only works in main thread," it indicates an attempt to set interrupt signals outside the main thread, something some libraries do unintentionally. This type of problem is solved by adjusting the way the application runs or moving sections of code that register signal handlers to the right location.

Flask's debug mode error display shows a traceback with the exact line where the exception occurred. In production, this traceback should not be exposed to the user as it may contain sensitive details, but in the development environment, it is essential to understand what failed. Viewing the call stack and identifying the function that triggered the failure facilitates immediate fixes. Activating debug is done with app.run(debug=True) or FLASK_DEBUG=1 in the terminal, but it is never recommended to use debug in production.

Python has a built-in breakpoint mode that stops execution and allows you to inspect variables. Inserting breakpoint() at critical points in the code, along with strategic prints, helps confirm values and logical flows. Another resource involves IDEs like Visual Studio Code or PyCharm, which offer visual debugging, setting breakpoints and examining the state of the application during each step. This process reveals logical errors such as loops that do not end or conditions that are never satisfied.

Logging enables retrospective analysis of a problem. When the service goes down or returns unexpected errors, the logs are the only source that describes what happened. Flask allows you to configure the writing of logs in the terminal or in files, in addition to integrating libraries such as logging, defining levels (DEBUG, INFO, WARNING, ERROR, CRITICAL) and message formats. In more elaborate projects, it is common to send these logs to observability platforms such as Elasticsearch, Splunk or specialized logging services. Thus, it becomes possible to search and correlate events over a period of time, locate error spikes or identify requests that preceded a serious failure.

The snippet below shows a minimal Python logging configuration, associated with Flask:

python

```
# EXAMPLE 1
# STEP 1: basic logging setup
import logging
from flask import Flask

app = Flask(__name__)

# STEP 2: define a logger with debug level
logging.basicConfig(level=logging.DEBUG, format='%(asctime)s [%(levelname)s] %(name)s: %(message)s')

@app.route("/")
def index():
    app.logger.debug("Index route accessed.")
    return "Hello from Flask!"

if __name__ == "__main__":
    app.run(debug=True)
```

The logging.basicConfig item configures the date/time format and the logging level, including displaying the logger name and message. When the index route is accessed, "Index route accessed." appears in the logs, next to the time and level. In complex situations, it is possible to create different loggers for each module, set specific levels and separate debug messages from genuine problems.

Routing errors occur when the application receives requests that were not handled by any route or when non-existent route parameters are called. If the route defines /user/int:user_id, but the URL accessed is /user/john, Flask returns 404 Not Found or aborts due to incorrect type. Confirming that the routes match the placeholder syntax and that each method (GET, POST, PUT, DELETE) is properly configured resolves most complaints.

Dependency conflicts occur when two libraries require different versions of the same package or when globally installed packages are mixed with packages from a virtual environment. This effect appears in logs as "ImportError: cannot import name 'X' from partially initialized module 'Y'," suggesting conflict or circular import. Checking the usage of a package manager, such as pipenv or poetry, unifies the installation and freezes versions in Pipfile.lock or poetry.lock, avoiding surprises. It is also recommended to isolate each project in a venv, preventing libraries from another project from interfering.

Config failures also appear if essential environment variables are not defined. In some applications, app.config["SECRET_KEY"] or app.config["DATABASE_URL"] depends on an .env or the production server. When they do not exist, the application does not start or behaves in an insecure manner. Checking whether Docker, Heroku or the platform in use is correctly injecting the variables is essential.

Hangs or timeouts can be more difficult to diagnose, as the application does not appear to crash, but is unresponsive. This could mean that there is an infinite loop or that some external call (such as requests.get) blocks waiting for a response from a down service. One way to locate the exact point of blocking is to use debug or insert logs in suspicious sections, for example, before and after each function call. If the second message never appears, you know which call stuck. In production, a time limit on the WSGI server (such as gunicorn) can abort the request if it exceeds a few seconds.

Performance issues require bottleneck analysis. In Flask, common factors are inefficient database queries, loops that process large volumes of data without paging, and inappropriate use of extensions that don't scale well. It is recommended to enter metrics to measure the time spent on each route, or employ a profiler that details how much time each function consumes. Tools like cProfile, pyinstrument or snakeviz allow you to map which part of the code consumes the most CPU. For I/O bottlenecks, adopting async with ASGI frameworks or configuring task queues for time-consuming processes alleviates the load on the main web service, responding to the user more quickly.

For optimizations, caches can be implemented: in some routes that generate static content or results that change little, the application stores the ready response for a period. This reduces redundant processing and access to the bank. Libraries like Flask-Caching support this process, storing the results in local memory or in Redis. Monitoring logs and metrics helps detect cache hits versus fallback hits (cache misses), evaluating whether the expiration policy is appropriate.

Some errors arise in extensions or middleware, for example, when using Flask-Login without defining the user_loader function, resulting in "NoneType object is not callable." Or if a blueprint has a duplicate route, Flask warns "View function mapping is overwriting an existing endpoint function." The messages describe the conflict, and the recommended action is to rename the roles, endpoints, or remove overlaps. Carefully reading the error message and searching for the implicated line of code almost always points to the solution.

The following snippet illustrates the endpoint overlap:

python

```python
# EXAMPLE 2
# STEP 1: blueprint definition
from flask import Blueprint

bp = Blueprint("main_bp", __name__)

@bp.route("/hello")
def hello():
    return "Hello from blueprint"

@bp.route("/hello")
def another_hello():
    return "Hello again"
```

In this code, both functions use @bp.route("/hello"), generating conflict. Flask's log says that the second route tries to overwrite the first. Just rename or change the path to / hello2, depending on the objective.

Library dependencies that depend on C-extensions, such as psycopg2 or uwsgi, may fail if there are no compilers or system packages installed. In logs, "gcc not found" or "No module named 'psycopg2' appears," but the real cause is the absence of dev packages on the system. In Docker containers, you need to install libpq-dev and gcc to compile psycopg2. On cloud servers, apt-get or yum solve part of the needs. The exact driver version may also be critical, as certain versions of psycopg2 do not support newer or inverted PostgreSQL functionality.

"UnicodeEncodeError" encoding conflicts appear when Flask generates responses with characters that cannot be encoded in the defined charset or when path strings contain accents without proper encoding. Ensuring that files and Python use UTF-8 usually does the trick. The adoption of from **future** import unicode_literals and checking that routes and templates work in UTF-8 are enough in most cases.

In the case of problems with circular import, the exception "ImportError: cannot import name X from partially initialized module Y" appears. Generally, one file imports another which, in turn, returns to the first. In Flask, this occurs if app.py imports something from routes.py, and routes.py also imports app.py. The solution involves reorganizing the project, perhaps defining the Flask instance in a factory or moving imports within the functions that depend on them, to reduce top-of-file interdependencies.

When investigating template issues, jinja2.exceptions.TemplateNotFound recurs when Flask cannot find the HTML file. This may result from a different path than expected or a missing file in the templates folder. Checking if the nomenclature matches what goes into render_template, and if the templates folder is in the root of the project or in a similar location to app/templates, helps to resolve this.

To resolve disagreements that only occur in production, enabling logging at lower levels on the WSGI server (gunicorn, uwsgi) and logging exceptions locally helps with correlation. Logging integrations can trigger alerts for every error 500 that the application returns, sending notification to services such as Sentry or Rollbar. This real-time monitoring is essential for critical systems as it detects anomalies immediately, enabling faster corrections.

SSL-related errors may include "ssl.SSLError: [SSL: WRONG_VERSION_NUMBER]" if the application attempts to establish an encrypted connection to an endpoint that does not speak TLS or if the port is incorrect. Correcting the server configuration or using http:// in the correct location usually resolves the issue. In proxy setups, such as NGINX or Apache, the encryption ends at the proxy and the connection to Flask continues over plain HTTP. Adjusting X-Forwarded-Proto headers and Flask-HTTPS settings may be necessary for the application to generate secure URLs.

Some large apps suffer from growing memory, as objects are retained, causing "MemoryError" or killing processes. A memory profiler in Python, such as pympler, helps detect if there is a cyclic reference or if data is not freed after requests. Investigating whether libraries retain caches that do not expire or whether there is a poorly designed infinite generator prevents this accumulation. In Docker containers, horizontal scaling can also dilute the load, but fixing the root of the problem is paramount.

CPU spikes or crashes may indicate loops that traverse millions of database records without paging or inefficient algorithms. Paginating results into smaller chunks and displaying only what the user needs eliminates excessive operations and memory load. It is also worth analyzing whether queries are repeated for each item in a loop, replacing them with a single query that already returns everything ready. APM (Application Performance Monitoring) tools analyze routes and display where time is spent, generating execution graphs.

In integrations with external APIs, timeouts and connection failures occur. The Flask application may be slow waiting for the response, blocking other requests if it is on a WSGI server with few workers. Introducing timeouts and fallback scenarios prevents the application from being held hostage by external services. For example, requests.get(url, timeout=5) throws an exception if there is no response within 5 seconds, allowing Flask to respond with an error message to the client instead of hanging indefinitely.

It is recommended to plan unit and integration tests to

exercise each route and each dependency, ensuring coverage of the main flows. When you push code that introduces a regression, these tests fail and indicate the culprit change. If a bug makes it into production, logs and monitoring help track the source.

For concurrency issues, if the application accesses external resources with simultaneous manipulations, crashes or race conditions may occur. Python, by the nature of the GIL, does not suffer much thread contention on the CPU, but simultaneous I/O requires care. When using parallel processes, objects in memory cannot be shared directly. Storing state to disk or in a central cache, using appropriate locks, resolves inconsistencies.

In terms of performance optimization, replacing Flask's native development server with a WSGI server like gunicorn or uwsgi is crucial for real-world loads. Configuring the appropriate number of workers and threads prevents saturation and takes advantage of available cores. In high-demand environments, balancing the application across multiple containers and distributing the load removes bottlenecks. Monitoring each route's latency and error rate helps you scale the number of instances needed.

Resolving conflicts and dependency errors in multi-tier scenarios requires a global view of how the application is deployed. Each continuous integration pipeline must install the same versions defined in the lock file, avoiding surprises. If a library X requires 2.0 and another requires 3.0 of the same package, you will need to find a version that meets both or migrate to a replacement. Looking closely at the error message generated in pip, you will usually find the mention of "Cannot install X because Y requires version <=2.0 but you have 3.0 installed." Adjusting the dependency solves it.

Some applications require import reordering to avoid partial initialization. If routes.py imports something from app.py, but app.py also imports something from routes.py, Flask may crash because the app is not fully defined when routes are loaded. A way around this is to use an application factory, in which a create_app function is created that instantiates and returns the application, and routes are registered within this function or imported after the app is created. Thus, the circular import is canceled, as the logic is executed in linear order.

As a last recommendation, discipline in the use of logs and the constant study of tracebacks help to resolve most errors in Flask. Confirming the existence and coherence of environment variables, checking the integrity of the virtual environment or container and observing error messages at startup greatly reduce the time spent on corrections. Testing whether the error is reproducible locally, and whether it appears in debug mode or only in production, directs the analysis of what differs between environments.

The troubleshooting domain allows Flask applications to evolve without becoming chaotic. A well-organized project, with logs at appropriate levels, versioned packages and clear startup scripts, means that most problems can be resolved quickly. Each error becomes an opportunity to improve the process and strengthen the application against similar failures in the future. Errors that would previously take hours to resolve can be tracked in minutes when there is visibility into the flow of requests, the internal state of the application and the deployment pipeline. This maturity in problem management and adoption of best practices makes Flask capable of dealing with both prototypes and crucial systems in corporate environments.

CHAPTER 12. INTRODUCTION TO FASTAPI

FastAPI has gained prominence in the Python ecosystem for its ability to create fast, asynchronous, and scalable APIs using static typing and efficient validations. This framework is based on Starlette and Pydantic, combining a high-performance asynchronous architecture with the ease of use typical of Python libraries. The proposal is to offer development of services and microservices with a focus on response speed, code readability and automated documentation. The set of these characteristics makes the process of creating routes and manipulating data simpler, without sacrificing quality or robustness.

FastAPI's philosophy is anchored in providing a fluid and productive development experience. Static typing and data validation happen through Pydantic models, which protects the application against unexpected values and silent failures. Routes defined with Python functions gain support for type annotations, and the framework uses this information to automatically generate interactive documentation in the OpenAPI standard (Swagger and Redoc). The use of async/await takes advantage of the benefits of the ASGI server, bringing improvements in scalability and the ability to handle simultaneous requests.

Installation and initial configuration are quite straightforward. In an environment with Python 3.7 or higher, simply get fastapi and an ASGI server (like uvicorn) to run the application. The language's advanced typing and coroutine-based concurrency model ensure that the same application can handle multiple requests at the same time, without blocking the main loop. This flow fits into modern scenarios, where microservices need to respond to calls from different customers quickly, and each route can query banks or external services without keeping the entire application stopped.

One of the most praised differences is the way FastAPI handles validation. Each parameter, whether route, query or body, can be annotated for typing. These types are converted into Pydantic models, which check values, guarantee limits, formats, and even transform data. The response to the customer is immediate when something is wrong, as the framework returns well-formatted validation errors, simplifying the identification of inconsistencies. This approach reduces code repetition as there is no need to write manual validators on each route.

To configure it, it is common to install the package and run uvicorn to serve the application. A first step might be:

bash

```
pip install fastapi uvicorn
```

Then a main file defines the routes:

python

```
# EXAMPLE 1
# STEP 1: basic app initialization
from fastapi import FastAPI

app = FastAPI()

# STEP 2: define a root endpoint
@app.get("/")
def read_root():
    return {"message": "Hello from FastAPI"}
```

```
# STEP 3: run with uvicorn (cli)
# uvicorn main:app --host 0.0.0.0 --port 8000
```

The FastAPI object is instantiated and receives routes via decorators. The read_root example matches a GET route on "/", returning a dictionary that is automatically serialized to JSON. The application can be run with uvicorn main:app, where main is the file name (without the .py extension) and app is the FastAPI object variable. On localhost:8000, this route displays { "message": "Hello from FastAPI" }.

A comparison between Flask and FastAPI reveals similar philosophies in the simplicity of routing, but with different focuses on execution. Flask is a microframework that offers great freedom without imposing additional styles or libraries. Adopting async in Flask requires extra configuration or separate libraries, while in FastAPI the idea of asynchronous functions is native. The validation flow in Flask tends to require extensions such as Flask-WTF or Marshmallow, while in FastAPI, typing with Pydantic replaces the approach of traditional configurators and validators.

Another point of distinction involves automatic documentation. In Flask, creating documentation relies on external libraries or manually writing specifications in the OpenAPI standard. In FastAPI, Pydantic class usage and type annotations automatically generate /docs and /redoc endpoints, displaying full descriptions of the routes, parameters, and expected responses. This functionality is advantageous for those who integrate third-party services or need to share the API with other teams.

The basic structure of a FastAPI application usually organizes each route as a function, decorated with @app.get, @app.post, @app.put or other HTTP methods. The framework also supports async def, allowing non-blocking asynchronous operations. This makes it possible to handle multiple requests without using traditional threads, reducing context overhead and offering high scalability. In high competition scenarios, adopting async generates performance advantages, as the application is not stopped during I/O waits.

Introducing route parameters follows the annotation pattern:

python

```
# EXAMPLE 2
# STEP 1: route with path parameter
@app.get("/users/{user_id}")
def read_user(user_id: int):
    return {"user_id": user_id}
```

When accessing /users/123, the user_id is converted to int, and the function receives this value. If the value is not a valid integer, FastAPI automatically returns a 422 Unprocessable Entity validation error, stating that "user_id" does not meet the criteria. This flow improves security and robustness.

Reading query parameters is done by indicating function parameters that are not in the path, but with default or non-default values:

python

```
# EXAMPLE 3
# STEP 1: route with query parameter
@app.get("/items")
def read_items(limit: int = 10, skip: int = 0):
    return {"limit": limit, "skip": skip}
```

Requests to /items?limit=5&skip=2 return JSON with limit=5 and skip=2. Typing ensures validation and conversion. If the user sends strings, the framework will try to convert, returning an error if it fails.

Request body handling in POST or PUT routes employs Pydantic models for validation. This method defines Python classes that describe each expected field, including its restrictions. When receiving JSON, FastAPI converts and validates everything before calling the function:

python

```
# EXAMPLE 4
# STEP 1: pydantic model
from pydantic import BaseModel

class UserCreate(BaseModel):
    username: str
    email: str
    is_active: bool = True

# STEP 2: route using the model
@app.post("/users")
def create_user(user: UserCreate):
    return {"msg": "User created", "data": user.dict()}
```

When sending a POST to /users with a JSON body in the form {"username": "alice", "email": "alice@example.com"}, user:UserCreate does the parsing and automatic validation. If email is not a string or is_active has an invalid type, the route fails, reporting the problem in detail. This style saves the need for if not field in request or manual checks.

The same Pydantic class can have advanced validators that check email formats, minimum lengths, regex and transformations. This extends to submodels that nest structures, enabling rich descriptions of complex payloads. This arrangement speeds up the creation of well-defined APIs, as contract errors stop before reaching the business logic.

FastAPI performance is based on ASGI uvicorn or hypercorn server. By default, uvicorn handles the event loop that dispatches requests. With each request, if the route is synchronous, the event is blocked until the response is ready. If the route is async and contains await, the loop can serve other requests while waiting for I/O, such as database queries or external calls. In systems with a large volume of accesses, this architecture makes the most of the cooperative nature of async, maintaining a high throughput rate with fewer resources.

Configuring the application in larger frameworks follows similar principles to frameworks like Flask. It is common to have a main file, other folders for routes, templates, services and configurations. In replacement of Blueprints, FastAPI offers APIRouter for grouping endpoints. This router defines a set of routes that can be set up in the main application, allowing you to modularize different areas of the system, such as /users and /products:

python

```python
# EXAMPLE 5
# STEP 1: user router
from fastapi import APIRouter

router = APIRouter()

@router.get("/profile")
def get_profile():
    return {"profile": "User profile data"}

# STEP 2: main app
from fastapi import FastAPI
from .user_router import router as user_router

app = FastAPI()

app.include_router(user_router, prefix="/users",
tags=["users"])
```

In the snippet, prefix="/users" makes /profile accessible from /users/profile. tags=["users"] serves for documentation, grouping routes related to the users resource. This modular method improves maintainability.

Automatic documentation is accessed by default in /docs (Swagger) and /redoc (Redoc). These endpoints allow you to test routes and visualize each parameter, facilitating collaboration with frontends or other services. You can customize titles, descriptions and examples. When defining the application, you can provide metadata to change the project title, version and contact information, reflected in the OpenAPI JSON.

A praised point in FastAPI is the ease of creating websockets for real-time communication. Thanks to the underlying Starlette, the application can define endpoints that accept WebSocket connections, sending and receiving asynchronous messages. This style is useful in chats, dashboards and collaborative apps. By uniting HTTP and WebSockets endpoints in the same framework, the project reduces the complexity of adopting separate servers.

The comparison with Flask, in terms of the community, shows that Flask has a huge user base, many extensions and material produced over the years. FastAPI, although newer, has grown quickly and attracts those who need high performance and automated documents. The two frameworks coexist well in the Python ecosystem, each meeting specific demands. Those who have already mastered Flask tend to learn FastAPI quickly, as the idea of decorators and routes is very similar. The biggest difference is in the typing and default use of async.

In terms of deployment, FastAPI requires an ASGI server. uvicorn and hypercorn are the usual choices, but some use daphne (from the Django Channels family). In Docker environments, the Dockerfile defines the installation of python, fastapi, uvicorn, and with docker run port 8000 is opened. In cloud providers, pointing to uvicorn main:app adjusts to serve connections. Scalability comes from instantiating multiple uvicorn workers or using a manager like gunicorn with uvicorn workers, which combines process scalability with asynchronous concurrency in each process.

Another key feature of FastAPI is handling security and authentication. It provides ready-made classes for OAuth2, Bearer tokens, and integrations with passwords and hashing. Declaring security parameters with Security and Depends generates endpoints that refuse requests if the token is not present. Thus, creating protected routes and roles becomes simpler. It is worth remembering that the framework does not impose a ready-made login system, but provides building blocks for JWT, OAuth or another method that meets the project's requirements.

Many projects use Pydantic not only for route inputs, but also to represent outputs or interact with databases. An item that is read from the database can be converted into a Pydantic model and returned to the client, maintaining uniformity in the structures. This custom avoids the "mess" of separate dictionaries and unformatted strings. By annotating each field with a type and descriptions, the application generates an OpenAPI dictionary that describes in detail which JSON is expected. It is common to see ModelIn and ModelOut classes, separating the input data shape and the output shape.

There is also the possibility of adding middleware to FastAPI to intercept requests before they reach routes or process responses before returning to the client. This pattern is useful for logging, compression, CORS or token verification. The Starlette API, which serves as the basis, offers decorators and classes to customize this behavior, as the request flow is subject to interception.

The fundamental structure of a larger project might include

an app directory, with subfolders such as routers, models, schemas, and a main.py that instantiates FastAPI and performs the include_router on each component. Each route is organized in your router, each Pydantic model in schemas, and each connection to the database can be in a services folder. This layout modularizes the code, allowing each team or each part of the project to evolve without confusing the rest.

A snippet exemplifying this arrangement:

plaintext

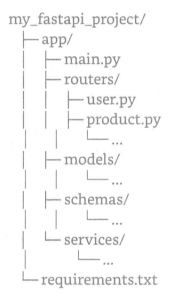

```
my_fastapi_project/
├── app/
│   ├── main.py
│   ├── routers/
│   │   ├── user.py
│   │   ├── product.py
│   │   │   └── ...
│   ├── models/
│   │   │   └── ...
│   ├── schemas/
│   │   │   └── ...
│   └── services/
│           └── ...
└── requirements.txt
```

main.py may contain:

python

```
# EXAMPLE 6
# STEP 1: main file
from fastapi import FastAPI
from .routers import user, product

app = FastAPI(title="My FastAPI Project", version="1.0.0")
```

```
app.include_router(user.router, prefix="/users",
tags=["Users"])
app.include_router(product.router, prefix="/products",
tags=["Products"])
```

user.py on routers defines user-specific endpoints, while product.py deals with products. In schemas, Pydantic classes model the inputs and outputs of each route. In models, if there is a relational database, the ORM classes can reside. The services folder brings together additional logic, such as email services or integrations with external APIs. This style guarantees maintainability and facilitates versioning, as each change tends to be concentrated in a thematic file or folder.

During development, uvicorn main:app --reload raises the server with automatic reload when detecting code changes. The workflow is agile: the developer creates or changes a route, saves it, and the server reboots in moments. The wide acceptance of FastAPI among the Python community is due to this simplicity combined with asynchronous power, robust typing and instantly generated documentation.

In terms of corporate use, the trend is to integrate FastAPI with databases such as PostgreSQL or NoSQL, defining repository packages and reusing Pydantic classes to check consistency. The adoption of Docker containers and Kubernetes orchestration fits well, as uvicorn has small overhead and starts quickly. In microsystems, each service can be a distinct FastAPI container, scaling as needed.

When planning an API with a focus on high performance, async's reactive approach avoids I/O blocks. If the application talks a lot with remote banks, external APIs or queues, each await releases the loop to process other requests. This makes FastAPI shine in high-throughput scenarios, compared to synchronous frameworks that require extra thread or worker configurations. However, for CPU-bound tasks, async alone does not solve the GIL, and it would be necessary to delegate to separate processes or use libraries such as multiprocessing.

The adoption of path operations, with standardized HTTP methods and annotations on status_code and responses, also enriches the routes. It's simple to declare specific returns such as status_code=201 for a POST that creates resources. The framework records this information in the documentation, making the API clearer. Route and doc remain together in the code, avoiding divergences between the actual implementation and what the doc says.

For those who want to customize the generation of documentation, it is possible to add descriptions, summaries, extra parameters and examples. This makes life easier for external consumers, who can test the API directly in the web interface generated by /docs. Swagger's Try it out function is very useful: just click, enter data and send, viewing the answer instantly. With this tool, endpoint validation and debugging is faster because you don't need to use external clients like Postman or cURL (although they are still popular in many streams).

Finally, the introduction to FastAPI highlights its flexibility: it is possible to start with a few lines and evolve into a complex application, distributed across multiple files and packages. The strongly typed approach, asynchronous execution and automatic documentation bring a modern API development model. The routing style with decorators, intuitive data manipulation and the extensibility of the Starlette ecosystem ensure that projects can grow without becoming bogged down.

The framework is attractive for teams that need to quickly deliver robust, documented and well-performing APIs. Support for websockets, background tasks and middleware integrates native facilities to build complete services. The community and active maintenance of the project reinforce the confidence of those who invest in the technology. In several comparisons, FastAPI shows results close to or better than famous tools in other languages, although actual performance depends on how the code handles I/O and takes advantage of async.

Among a universe of Python libraries for web development, FastAPI stands out for its pragmatism, adoption of modern resources and simplicity of use. The learning curve is not steep for those who know Python, and adding features such as annotations and coroutines proves to be fluid. Many developers who have migrated from synchronous frameworks report gains in readability, speed, and reduced validation bugs. Official support for Python 3.7+ and compliance with typing PEPs show the project's alignment with language trends.

Therefore, the fundamental point of the entire process is to understand that an ASGI server, the use of async/await and the combination with Pydantic form a powerful trio. The application has routes defined by decorators, each route takes advantage of type annotations to generate doc and validate parameters, and the server executes functions concurrently. Those who are used to working with Flask will notice similarities in the style of decorators, but will notice differences when handling async and dealing with the sophisticated validation scheme. This model represents a solid option for medium to large APIs and services, especially in architectures that prioritize scalability and robustness.

CHAPTER 13. CREATING APIS WITH FASTAPI

Developers seek to create interfaces that allow communication between different systems in a reliable and efficient way. One of the modern approaches to achieving this goal is based on creating APIs following RESTful standards or similar architectures, where each route manipulates resources and parameters. FastAPI offers advanced features for handling requests and responses, data validation and automatic documentation, without requiring extra configuration. The main focus is on performance and clarity, thanks to the combination of static typing, Pydantic and Starlette. This set facilitates the construction of scalable services, making the development process simpler and safer.

The definition and creation of endpoints starts with the FastAPI instance, which receives decorators for each route. HTTP methods can be used to organize different types of operations, such as GET, POST, PUT and DELETE. The behavior and validation of each endpoint becomes predictable, as each function writes down its parameters and return. The asynchronous environment allows the application to serve several requests at the same time, avoiding blocking during input and output operations.

A startup script can illustrate how to define a minimal API, already capable of handling HTTP requests:

python

```
# EXAMPLE 1
# PASSO 1: importing the necessary modules
```

```python
from fastapi import FastAPI

# STEP 2: creating the FastAPI instance
app = FastAPI()

# PASSO 3: defining a simple GET endpoint
@app.get("/")
def read_root():
    return {"message": "Welcome to the API"}

# PASSO 4: running with uvicorn
# uvicorn main:app --reload
```

The snippet above contains a single route to GET at the root. When accessing "/", the server returns a dictionary serialized as JSON. The default host is 127.0.0.1 and port 8000 if uvicorn is invoked without additional parameters. The --reload parameter triggers automatic reloading when the code is modified.

Handling requests and responses can go beyond returning simple dictionaries. FastAPI supports the definition of Pydantic classes that describe the structure of the expected or returned data, as well as the explicit configuration of status codes and headers. Python functions can receive Request objects to inspect header and cookie metadata, returning Response objects to customize status and body.

An excerpt demonstrating how to send specific JSON and custom headers:

python

```python
# EXAMPLE 2
# STEP 1: import modules for request, response, status
from fastapi import FastAPI, Response, status

app = FastAPI()
```

```python
@app.post("/items")
def create_item(response: Response):
    response.status_code = status.HTTP_201_CREATED
    response.headers["Custom-Header"] = "MyValue"
    return {"detail": "Item created successfully"}
```

response.status_code defines the HTTP status code to be sent, and response.headers adds headers. In default mode, the function would return 200 OK, but here the route defines 201 Created to indicate the creation of a resource.

Route parameters and query strings allow you to capture values that influence the endpoint logic. In FastAPI, any part enclosed in braces { } in the path represents a route variable. The framework automatically converts the type if an annotation is specified. Query strings are optional parameters that appear after "?", and can be defined with default or non-default values to make them mandatory.

An example that displays the definition of both:

python

```python
# EXAMPLE 3
# STEP 1: route with path parameter and query
from fastapi import FastAPI

app = FastAPI()

@app.get("/users/{user_id}")
def read_user(user_id: int, active_only: bool = True):
    return {"user_id": user_id, "active_only": active_only}
```

When accessing /users/10?active_only=false, the user_id becomes 10 (int) and the active_only becomes False (bool), thanks to the automatic converter. If something invalid like user_id=abc is sent, the framework returns a

422 Unprocessable Entity validation error. Handling route parameters and query strings does not require manual validations, as FastAPI does them using the declared types.

To deal with complex requests, the adoption of Pydantic models is essential. When describing a request body, the route defines a parameter that receives an object of type BaseModel. This object validates fields, types and formats, returning a structured error in case of failure. The workflow becomes reliable: the application guarantees that the received data meets the schema and, if correct, the route proceeds without extra checks.

A Pydantic model and endpoint for creating resources:

python

```
# EXAMPLE 4
# STEP 1: import from pydantic
from pydantic import BaseModel

class Item(BaseModel):
    name: str
    description: str | None = None
    price: float

@app.post("/items")
def create_item(item: Item):
    return {"result": "Item created", "item_data": item.dict()}
```

When receiving a JSON like {"name": "Laptop", "price": 1299.99}, the framework converts it to an item object: Item. If the price for string or name field is missing, validation fails and the response reaches the client in the form of JSON containing error details. This behavior avoids typing problems and data gaps that could spread throughout the application.

The function return is also transformed into JSON. If you want specific status codes, you can use the syntax:

python

```python
# EXAMPLE 5
# STEP 1: custom status code
from fastapi import status

@app.post("/items",
status_code=status.HTTP_201_CREATED)
def create_item(item: Item):
    return {"msg": "Item created", "data": item.dict()}
```

This style clarifies that the route returns 201 Created. You can also return objects of type Response, but the above way is the most common and idiomatic.

API development with FastAPI features automatic documentation in /docs (Swagger) and /redoc (Redoc) endpoints. Everything that is defined in the typing and routes appears in these interactive panels, where it is possible to test each call, insert parameters and check results. This feature speeds up integration with clients, whether frontends or other microservices. Leaving the trivial route and moving on to more complete cases involves introducing additional routes and grouping logic, possibly with APIRouter.

An example router, separating endpoints from users:

python

```python
# EXAMPLE 6
# STEP 1: create a user router
from fastapi import APIRouter
from pydantic import BaseModel

router = APIRouter()

class User(BaseModel):
    username: str
```

```
    email: str
    active: bool = True

@router.get("/list")
def list_users():
    return {"users": ["alice", "bob", "charlie"]}

@router.post("/new")
def create_user(user: User):
    return {"msg": "User created", "user_data": user.dict()}
```

In main.py, the central application can import this router and register it:

python

```
# EXAMPLE 7
# STEP 1: main app
from fastapi import FastAPI
from .user_router import router as user_router

app = FastAPI()

app.include_router(user_router, prefix="/users",
tags=["users"])

@app.get("/")
def root():
    return {"message": "API up and running"}
```

The list_users and create_user routes are accessible in / users/list and /users/new, carrying the prefix. Tag usage is for documentation, grouping these endpoints as part of the "users" set. Modularization avoids confusion when the project scales, allowing each domain (orders, products, authentication) to have its own router.

Handling HTTP methods and sending custom responses

makes the API more expressive. A PUT endpoint that updates a resource may require the ID in the route and the body with data:

python

```python
# EXAMPLE 8
# STEP 1: update route
@app.put("/items/{item_id}")
def update_item(item_id: int, item: Item):
    return {
        "message": "Item updated",
        "item_id": item_id,
        "updated_data": item.dict()
    }
```

This route extracts item_id from path and item from body, both validated. In real scenarios, you could search for the item in the bank, apply modifications and return the result. If item_id does not exist, an error or other form of flag could be returned.

Using async def allows non-blocking I/O handling. In network or bank intensive scripts, the application can manage several simultaneous connections:

python

```python
# EXAMPLE 9
# STEP 1: asynchronous route
import httpx

@app.get("/external")
async def call_external():
    async with httpx.AsyncClient() as client:
        r = await client.get("https://api.example.com/data")
        return r.json()
```

Here, when waiting for the response from the HTTP client, the Python event loop takes care of other requests, instead of sitting idle. This scalable model is one of the biggest highlights of FastAPI, enabling high throughput for services that depend on multiple calls to external APIs or asynchronous databases.

Adopting dependencies, through Depends, introduces another way to create well-structured APIs. A method defines the logic for checking authentication tokens or extracting bank connections, and each route declares a dependency that will be executed before handing over control. This approach generates clean and testable code, as routes focus on their operations, while authentication, or the manipulation of external resources, remains isolated.

An example of a dependency to check tokens:

python

```
# EXAMPLE 10
# STEP 1: a function that raises an exception if token is invalid
from fastapi import Depends, HTTPException, status

def verify_token(token: str):
    if token != "supersecrettoken":
        raise
HTTPException(status_code=status.HTTP_401_UNAUTHORIZED, detail="Invalid token")
    return token

@app.get("/secure")
def secure_endpoint(token: str = Depends(verify_token)):
    return {"message": "Access granted"}
```

If the token is other than "supersecrettoken," the verify_token function throws HTTPException. The secure_endpoint route receives token as a parameter, but does not need to check anything: Depends has already guaranteed validation. This technique becomes essential in large applications, as the logic for checking credentials, logs, rate-limiting or service injection can be centralized.

The introduction of query strings and search filters is another essential point in APIs:

python

```
# EXAMPLE 11
# STEP 1: listing items with optional filtering
@app.get("/products")
def list_products(skip: int = 0, limit: int = 10, search: str | None = None):
    # hypothetical data
    all_products = [
        {"id": 1, "name": "Laptop"},
        {"id": 2, "name": "Mouse"},
        {"id": 3, "name": "Monitor"},
        # ...
    ]
    if search:
        filtered = [p for p in all_products if search.lower() in p["name"].lower()]
    else:
        filtered = all_products

    return filtered[skip: skip + limit]
```

This endpoint applies skip and limit to page results, and search to filter by name. Annotations define the type and default value, so if skip or limit are not passed, 0 and 10 will be used. The framework converts search to None if there is no value, and booleans if it was a boolean field. With this, the route can handle inputs without manual checks, benefiting from the built-in validation and conversion system.

In APIs with routes that return lists, displaying pagination metadata helps consumers know how many total records there are, which page is current, and how many items are left. The application may return something like:

python

```python
# EXAMPLE 12
# STEP 1: return metadata and data
@app.get("/products")
def list_products(skip: int = 0, limit: int = 10):
    data = [
        {"id": 1, "name": "Laptop"},
        {"id": 2, "name": "Mouse"},
        {"id": 3, "name": "Monitor"},
        {"id": 4, "name": "Keyboard"},
        # ...
    ]
    total = len(data)
    return {
        "total": total,
        "skip": skip,
        "limit": limit,
        "results": data[skip: skip + limit]
    }
```

This style standardizes the way of returning collections, making life easier for those who consume the API, as the application not only returns the subset but also informs how many items there are in total.

Another common use of APIs with FastAPI is documentation of practical examples. You can provide example payloads for each route, which will appear in the /docs interface. This quickly teaches you how to call the route and what data to expect. For example, for the item creation endpoint:

python

```
# EXAMPLE 13
# STEP 1: usage of docstrings and examples
@app.post("/items", response_description="Create a new
item")
def create_item(
    item: Item = Body(
        ...,
        examples={
            "normal": {
                "summary": "A normal example",
                "description": "A normal item with name and
price",
                "value": {
                    "name": "iPhone",
                    "description": "Apple smartphone",
                    "price": 999.99
                }
            }
        }
    )
):
    return {"message": "Item created", "item_data": item.dict()}
```

Body(...) receives the examples option, which defines a dictionary with possible scenarios. This snippet generates a dropdown of examples in the Swagger documentation, allowing the user to click and automatically fill in the request body with the fields. This feature reduces ambiguities, especially when working with more complex or nested structures.

The request and response handling flow also extends to the use of middleware. FastAPI, through the underlying Starlette, allows you to register functions that intercept requests before and after calling the route. This style is applied for logging, compression or generic authentication:

python

```python
# EXAMPLE 14
# STEP 1: define a middleware
from starlette.requests import Request
from starlette.responses import Response

@app.middleware("http")
async def log_requests(request: Request, call_next):
    print(f"Request path: {request.url.path}")
    response = await call_next(request)
    print(f"Response status: {response.status_code}")
    return response
```

This middleware prints the path and, after processing the route, the status. It's a simple way to understand the flow of requests without repeating prints in each function.

Creating robust APIs can also include custom exception handling. If you need to return a specific error format or deal with database exceptions, you define handlers with the app.exception_handler() annotation:

python

```python
# EXAMPLE 15
# STEP 1: handle a custom exception
class MyCustomError(Exception):
    def __init__(self, detail: str):
        self.detail = detail

@app.exception_handler(MyCustomError)
async def custom_error_handler(request: Request, exc:
MyCustomError):
    return JSONResponse(
```

```
    status_code=400,
    content={"error": exc.detail},
)
```

If the route throws MyCustomError("Invalid operation"), the custom_error_handler function is invoked, returning JSON with status 400. This centralized design keeps the code clean and standardizes the error structure without spreading formatting logic all over the place.

Manipulation of data in format other than JSON, such as text/plain or file uploads, is also supported. When receiving uploads, the route notes File and UploadFile, and when returning files, you can use Starlette classes such as FileResponse. The goal is to cover all the needs of a modern API, including when the need arises for routes that return binaries or images.

An example of a route that receives files:

python

```python
# EXAMPLE 16
# STEP 1: receive file uploads
from fastapi import File, UploadFile

@app.post("/upload")
async def upload_file(file: UploadFile = File(...)):
    contents = await file.read()
    return {"filename": file.filename, "size": len(contents)}
```

The upload uses form data in the body, and File(...) tells FastAPI that this parameter comes from a file type field. The UploadFile contains metadata such as filename, content_type, and methods to read or write its content without storing everything in memory, depending on the configuration. This flow covers image, document and backup manipulation scenarios.

As a way to exemplify versatility, it is feasible to create routes for third-party APIs, combining the async approach and transforming responses. If the application is a gateway or orchestrates calls to several microservices, the syntax does not differ much: just use an asynchronous HTTP client and return the data in the convenient format.

A route that calls another service and concatenates data:

python

```
# EXAMPLE 17
# STEP 1: external call
import httpx

@app.get("/aggregate")
async def aggregate():
    async with httpx.AsyncClient() as client:
        users_resp = await client.get("https://api.example.com/users")
        products_resp = await client.get("https://api.example.com/products")

    users_data = users_resp.json()
    products_data = products_resp.json()
    return {"users_count": len(users_data), "products_count": len(products_data)}
```

When accessing /aggregate, the application makes two parallel calls and adds results, returning something simple. This style sets the foundation for service integrations and compositions without locking the loop during remote operations.

With these examples, a comprehensive view of how to design APIs with the framework is created, from simple routes to scenarios that include payload validation, query string manipulation and request interception. Performance is favored by the asynchronous mode and the lightness of the underlying Starlette, while security and consistency derive from Pydantic and the automatic error and doc facilities.

Adopting conventions, such as always returning JSON in the format { "data": ..., "error": ... } or { "message": ..., "payload": ... }, also provides uniformity. FastAPI's documentation generator highlights each parameter and schema, helping those who consume the API. In a larger team, this feature reduces ambiguities, as the doc stays synchronized with the code in real time.

Adding logs and monitoring is done using loggers or middleware, and robustness against errors is achieved by defining exception handlers and taking advantage of Python's typing to block inappropriate inputs. If it is necessary to increase the validation level, Pydantic is expanded with validators, regex and value constraints, minimizing failures and potential attacks.

With the approach described, any project benefits, whether for rapid prototypes or for production systems that need high scalability and data compliance. Best practices include splitting the API into modules (APIRouter) per domain, organizing Pydantic models in a clear place, and leveraging annotations to keep code clean. The use of environment variables for configurations and the adoption of Docker and uvicorn on multiple workers complete a solid deployment stack.

Therefore, when creating APIs with FastAPI, each route is expressed as a decorated Python function, which handles strongly typed inputs and outputs. This clarity speeds development and reduces errors, supported by competitive performance and embedded documentation. The handling of requests and responses flows naturally, without rework to convert data, and the query strings and route parameters follow the same typed logic. Thus, the creation of incremental, practical and easily maintained services becomes feasible in a dynamic language like Python, demonstrating the strength of asynchronous techniques and advanced typing.

CHAPTER 14. TYPING AND VALIDATION WITH PYDANTIC

Developers of APIs and web services face constant challenges when handling data coming from customers, banks or other external sources. Information may be incomplete, malformed or contain unexpected types, causing failures that are only detected at run time or, even worse, in production. Pydantic appears as a tool that combines the power of Python's static typing with automatic data validation, preventing errors from spreading and ensuring greater reliability in the code. FastAPI leans heavily on this concept, using type annotations to convert and verify route parameters, query strings, and request bodies.

The introduction to Pydantic and data models begins with the understanding that this library is not limited to one-off validations. The classes that inherit from BaseModel become the center of defining the structures accepted or returned by the application, containing not only the types of each field, but also additional behaviors, such as restrictions, default values and even pre- and post-processing methods. Python 3.7 or higher, which supports more modern annotations, makes adopting this approach even easier.

The snippet below demonstrates how to create a basic model to represent items in a commerce system:

python

```
# EXAMPLE 1
# STEP 1: import from pydantic
from pydantic import BaseModel
```

```
class Item(BaseModel):
    name: str
    price: float
    description: str | None = None
    in_stock: bool = True
```

The Item class defines the name, price, description and in_stock fields with concrete types. If the application receives JSON that matches this model, Pydantic converts each value and checks that they follow the type annotations. If deserialization fails, the error is reported in a structured way, pointing out which field is incorrect and why. The description param is optional as it is noted as str | None, and in_stock sets a default value of True. This strategy eliminates the need to manually check whether the request included a certain field or whether its type matches what was expected.

The benefits of static typing in FastAPI appear clearly when routes use these templates as parameters. Each endpoint defines the model for input (or output), and the framework handles the conversion and validation. This process applies to both POST and PUT routes, which require request bodies, as well as query strings and path parameters. Using annotations, for example name:str, ensures that if the user sends an integer instead of a string, the error is identified immediately.

An endpoint that receives a body of type Item and returns a response:

python

```
# EXAMPLE 2
# STEP 1: import and define the FastAPI app
from fastapi import FastAPI
from pydantic import BaseModel

app = FastAPI()
```

```python
class Item(BaseModel):
    name: str
    price: float

@app.post("/items")
def create_item(item: Item):
    return {"msg": "Item created", "item_data": item.dict()}
```

The @app.post decorator says that this endpoint processes POST requests in the /items path. The create_item function receives item: Item, and FastAPI extracts the values from the JSON present in the body. Typing automatically defines validation and, if something diverges from the schema, the response returns with status 422 and a body describing the error. This prevents the application from having to manually program to check the type or presence of each field.

Automatic data validation protects against inconsistencies and malicious attacks that attempt to send invalid payloads. If price is string or name is missing, the framework blocks the request. Instead of silently collapsing on exceptions or writing erroneous data to the database, the application informs the client that the format does not meet the requirements. This screening mechanism is a crucial step towards robust APIs.

Pydantic goes beyond simple type checking by offering additional validators and configurations. Classes can define restrictions such as minimum lengths, numeric ranges, or field formatting. For email addresses, the library includes EmailStr, which checks whether the value follows the email pattern. For strings that must conform to a regex, the Field class accepts regex parameters and size impositions. An example of more advanced settings:

python

EXAMPLE 3

```python
# STEP 1: advanced model with validations
from pydantic import BaseModel, Field, EmailStr

class User(BaseModel):
    username: str = Field(..., min_length=3, max_length=50)
    email: EmailStr
    age: int = Field(..., gt=0, lt=150)
    bio: str | None = Field(default=None, max_length=200)
```

The username must be 3 to 50 characters long, age must be greater than 0 and less than 150. The bio field is optional, but if provided, it cannot exceed 200 characters. Email uses EmailStr to validate the structure. If the JSON does not comply with these rules, the route rejects the request. This degree of protection saves later rework, as it ensures that routes only receive coherent data. Routes using this User can assume age is a valid number and email follows the email pattern, simplifying the internal logic.

Practical application cases occur anywhere in the data flow. If the system sends responses that must follow a format, the routes can return Pydantic templates, and FastAPI converts the object to JSON. This method standardizes outputs, maintaining compatibility and avoiding missing fields. In applications that distribute data to multiple clients, this consistency brings major gains in trust.

An endpoint that returns a User object:

python

```python
# EXAMPLE 4
# STEP 1: define user schema
class User(BaseModel):
    username: str
    email: EmailStr

@app.get("/users/{user_id}", response_model=User)
```

```
def get_user(user_id: int):
    # hypothetical retrieval
    data = {"username": "alice", "email": "alice@example.com"}
    return data
```

The response_model=User parameter indicates that the route returns something in the format of the User class. If the returned dictionary does not fit perfectly (for example, missing email), FastAPI generates an error. This final check prevents the absence of an essential field due to carelessness or the return of another field that the doc does not mention.

Another powerful aspect of Pydantic is the ability to pre- and post-process data using validation methods. The library allows you to create specific validators that run before setting the value of a field or after, adjusting or checking consistency between fields. This feature becomes useful if the application needs, for example, to ensure that the sum of two fields does not exceed a certain limit or that an end_date field is later than the start_date. The snippet:

python

```
# EXAMPLE 5
# STEP 1: custom validator
from pydantic import BaseModel, validator
from datetime import date

class Event(BaseModel):
    name: str
    start_date: date
    end_date: date

    @validator("end_date")
    def check_dates(cls, v, values):
        start = values.get("start_date")
        if start and v < start:
```

```
    raise ValueError("end_date must be after start_date")
return v
```

The check_dates function runs every time end_date is read, checking if end_date >= start_date. If not, it raises ValueError, which Pydantic converts to a validation error. Thus, the application is protected from records where an event ends before it begins. In booking, schedule, and calendar APIs, this feature is valuable for ensuring data integrity.

Pydantic supports model inheritance, making it possible to compose broader data structures. You can create nested submodels, such as the Address class for address data, and the UserProfile class that includes address: Address. This design distributes responsibilities and simplifies maintenance, as each sub-block validates itself independently. When returning or receiving complex objects, the application maintains coherence and reuses validations in different contexts.

A logging or tracing scenario exemplifies the advantage of static typing. If a route requires the user to enter param user_id: int, but the caller sends user_id: "abc," the failure would be detected immediately, saving the API from dealing with inappropriate strings. In a solution without Pydantic, the programmer could discover this failure only at runtime, or deal with it manually with if type(...) checks. Pydantic relieves you of this burden and generates clear reports of where and how the conversion failed.

Another strength of Pydantic is datetime modeling using Python datetime. When receiving dates in ISO 8601 format, the application automatically converts the string into datetime objects, generating an error if the syntax is incorrect. When dealing with time zones, Pydantic settings can be adjusted, and the route validates whether the date is timezone aware or not. This care avoids confusion that could arise when dates are mixed with arbitrary values.

In the context of FastAPI, the adoption of Pydantic and static typing also extends to route, query and header parameters. It is possible to define, for example, classes that describe multiple query parameters, using the FastAPI dependency:

python

```
# EXAMPLE 6
# STEP 1: query model
from fastapi import Depends

class FilterOptions(BaseModel):
    search: str | None = None
    limit: int = 10
    offset: int = 0

def get_filters(
    search: str | None = None,
    limit: int = 10,
    offset: int = 0
):
    return FilterOptions(search=search, limit=limit, offset=offset)

@app.get("/items")
def list_items(filters: FilterOptions = Depends(get_filters)):
    # filters is a validated instance
    # hypothetical data
    return {
        "search": filters.search,
        "limit": filters.limit,
        "offset": filters.offset
    }
```

In this mechanism, the get_filters function reads query parameters and constructs a FilterOptions. The BaseModel constructor does the necessary checking and conversion. If search must be string or None, and limit must be integer, the route does not need to repeat validation. list_items receives filters as an already coherent object. This style injects typing and validation logic without polluting each individual route. In large projects, this approach avoids redundancy in routes that share similar parameters.

In applications that involve creating multiple records, Pydantic helps manage lists of objects. A route that inserts multiple items might use:

python

```
# EXAMPLE 7
# STEP 1: batch insertion
from typing import List

@app.post("/batch/items")
def batch_create_items(items: List[Item]):
    return {"created_count": len(items), "items": [i.dict() for i in
items]}
```

The items: List[Item] defines that the body must be a JSON array, each validated as an Item. If any item fails, the entire request is marked as invalid. In some situations, the application may want partial validation, but the default behavior is to refuse everything if an object in the list does not fit.

The ability to realign data also shines when receiving field names that differ from what the application wants to use internally. Pydantic provides alias arguments to map a JSON field to a Python property:

python

```
# EXAMPLE 8
# STEP 1: alias usage
```

```python
class Article(BaseModel):
    title: str = Field(alias="headline")
    body: str = Field(alias="content")

@app.post("/articles")
def create_article(article: Article):
    return {
        "title": article.title,
        "body": article.body
    }
```

If the JSON comes with "headline" and "content," the Article template automatically maps to title and body, but in internal Python, it uses those names. This trick is useful when the API needs to maintain compatibility with a client that already adopts a different nomenclature or some legacy standard.

For cases where the application returns data in large volumes, defining response_model in the route decorator orchestrates the conversion back to Pydantic format. Thus, the generated JSON follows the template pattern. If the route returns sensitive columns, you can create a derived model without these fields, ensuring that information does not leak. Pydantic then becomes the single point of configuration for both input and output data, enhancing security and clarity of purpose.

Pydantic's flexibility is also evident in scenarios where complex formats need to be converted, for example, when receiving nested data. Consider a shopping cart with several items and a calculated subtotal:

python

```python
# EXAMPLE 9
# STEP 1: nested models
class CartItem(BaseModel):
    product_id: int
    quantity: int
```

```
    price: float
class Cart(BaseModel):
    user_id: int
    items: list[CartItem]
    subtotal: float

@app.post("/cart")
def create_cart(cart: Cart):
    return {"message": "Cart created", "cart": cart.dict()}
```

If the request sends a JSON containing user_id, items and subtotal, each CartItem will be validated individually, ensuring that product_id and quantity are integers and price is a float. If any item breaks the rules, validation fails globally. This way, the application is sure that if the create_cart function is called, all objects in the cart are consistent.

A notable point is the performance. Although Pydantic does additional conversions and checks, its efficient Cython design and internal cache enable high validation speed. In many benchmarks, performance satisfies most production loads. The additional overhead offsets the huge gain in reliability and bug reduction. If the API serves millions of requests, there are still ways to optimize or use partial models, but in most cases, adopting Pydantic fits smoothly.

When talking about practical application cases, it is common to see Pydantic combined with databases. A GET route reads data from the database, converts it to a dictionary and returns a Pydantic model, or the reverse to insert records. Tools like SQLAlchemy define ORM classes, and Pydantic classes define the input and output contract. You can map the ORM to Pydantic and vice versa, preventing invalid data from reaching the repository.

A manipulation flow with ORM and Pydantic:

python

```python
# EXAMPLE 10
# STEP 1: SQLAlchemy model
from sqlalchemy import Column, Integer, String
from sqlalchemy.ext.declarative import declarative_base

Base = declarative_base()

class UserDB(Base):
    __tablename__ = "users"
    id = Column(Integer, primary_key=True, index=True)
    username = Column(String, unique=True)
    email = Column(String, unique=True)

# STEP 2: Pydantic model
class UserCreate(BaseModel):
    username: str
    email: EmailStr

@app.post("/users")
def create_user(user: UserCreate, db: Session =
Depends(get_db)):
    user_db = UserDB(username=user.username,
email=user.email)
    db.add(user_db)
    db.commit()
    db.refresh(user_db)
    return {"message": "User created", "id": user_db.id}
```

The UserDB class reflects the table in the database, while UserCreate defines the payload that the route accepts. If the JSON does not have a username or email, or if the email is invalid, the route fails immediately, preserving the integrity of the database. This design ensures that the backend maintains coherence and returns immediate feedback to whoever consumed the endpoint.

There are also Pydantic features for transforming values, such as lowercasing strings or generating defaults with functions. If a field demands timestamp, the model can create auto_now:

python

```
# EXAMPLE 11
# STEP 1: auto now
from pydantic import BaseModel, Field
from datetime import datetime

class LogEntry(BaseModel):
    timestamp: datetime =
Field(default_factory=datetime.utcnow)
    level: str
    message: str
```

The Field(default_factory=...) indicates that each instance generates a current timestamp. So the route doesn't have to worry about manually entering this value. In logs or audits, it saves effort, as every log already comes with a date. At the time JSON is parsed, if timestamp is not provided, default_factory calls datetime.utcnow.

Another practical case is password manipulation and hashing. The route can accept a password, but not store it as is. Pydantic's validator calls a hashing function and substitutes this value:

python

```
# EXAMPLE 12
# STEP 1: hashing password in Pydantic
from pydantic import BaseModel, validator

def hash_password(raw: str) -> str:
    # hypothetical hashing function
    return "hashed_" + raw
```

```
class UserRegistration(BaseModel):
    username: str
    password: str

    @validator("password")
    def hash_pwd(cls, v):
        return hash_password(v)

@app.post("/register")
def register_user(data: UserRegistration):
    return {"user": data.username, "pwd_hash": data.password}
```

hash_pwd replaces the password field with the hashing result. Whoever calls the register_user function receives the string "hashed_original" instead of the password, preventing the route from having to write this hash manually. The class centralizes the logic, facilitating maintenance and preventing direct access to the pure password.

Pydantic also manages aliases and extra fields. In some APIs, the consumer sends snake_case, but the internal application uses camelCase, or vice versa. There are settings to automatically convert one style to another, ensuring compatibility. This alias_generator feature adjusts each attribute and saves alias repetition across all fields.

Finally, in the context of FastAPI, the adoption of these practices enriches the development experience, as the interactive doc clearly displays which fields exist in each model, which are optional, which have default and which types are expected. The valuable check prevents errors from propagating to the database, caches, or other microservices. In applications that communicate with front-ends, immediate feedback in the case of invalid data speeds client-side remediation, and Pydantic's consistency of use across endpoints ensures that the application maintains a uniform

API.

In summary, typing and validation with Pydantic provides a solid foundation for managing reliable data in Python, especially in FastAPI applications. Each route explicitly informs the structures it accepts and returns, each field receives an exact type, and automatic validations handle consistency. This approach considerably reduces the likelihood of bugs related to types or formats, speeds up development thanks to automatic documentation and frees the team from manual and repetitive checks. The robustness of this ecosystem makes FastAPI APIs more predictable, secure and simple to evolve, integrating with banks, external services and complex structures without compromising clarity.

CHAPTER 15. AUTOMATIC DOCUMENTATION WITH FASTAPI

Projects that make APIs available for consumption by internal teams or external partners face a major challenge in clarifying and maintaining specifications. FastAPI stands out by automatically generating documentation, interactively displaying routes, parameters, request bodies and expected responses. This functionality reduces the need to write specifications manually, as the framework reads Pydantic type annotations and classes to produce an OpenAPI-compliant document. Professionals using the API gain efficiency by consulting a panel to test each route, inspect models, and check for common errors.

Interactive documentation generation uses two main interfaces: Swagger and Redoc. By default, FastAPI exposes the /docs route, which presents the Swagger UI interface, and the /redoc route, which presents the ReDoc interface. Both interpret the automatically generated OpenAPI file, including endpoints, HTTP methods, route and query parameters, as well as data models. The developer does not need to install extra libraries for this part, as it is already part of the main package, as long as the application runs in normal mode with FastAPI and an ASGI server like uvicorn.

The experience becomes simple for anyone who wants to explore the API. Just launch the application and visit /docs. The screen shows a list of endpoints with their descriptions, parameters, input and output formats, and possible status codes. There is also a button that allows you to test the call in the browser itself, sending data, capturing the response and displaying headers and body. This approach replaces the need for additional tools such as cURL or Postman, particularly in the early stages of development. Technical users can interact with the API and understand the behavior of each route.

The following snippet offers a minimal view of how a developer launches an application and relies on interactive documentation:

python

```python
# EXAMPLE 1
# STEP 1: create a FastAPI instance
from fastapi import FastAPI
from pydantic import BaseModel

app = FastAPI()

# STEP 2: define a data model
class Item(BaseModel):
    name: str
    price: float

# STEP 3: define a route that creates items
@app.post("/items")
def create_item(item: Item):
    return {"msg": "Item created", "item": item.dict()}

# STEP 4: run the server with uvicorn
# uvicorn main:app --reload
```

Visiting /docs it is possible to see the /items route of type POST, displaying the expected body as an Item object, with name and price. Any change to the model or route is immediately reflected in the documentation. This keeps the content synchronized and prevents discrepancies between what is implemented and what is described.

Customizing your API documentation allows you to adjust the title, description, and contact information. It is common to want to display, at the top of the interface, a project name, version and a general explanation. This care facilitates adoption by other teams. The OpenAPI file is generated from the metadata provided when constructing the FastAPI object. An illustrative code:

python

```
# EXAMPLE 2
# STEP 1: configure metadata
app = FastAPI(
    title="Inventory Service API",
    description="Manages items and stocks in the inventory
system",
    version="2.3.0",
    contact={
        "name": "Support Team",
        "url": "https://company.example.com/support",
        "email": "support@company.example.com"
    }
)

@app.get("/health")
def health_check():
    return {"status": "ok"}
```

/docs displays "Inventory Service API" as the title, "Manages items and stocks in the inventory system" as the general description, and the contact section at the bottom. This layout is also reflected in the OpenAPI JSON file, which is located in the /openapi.json route by default. The Redoc interface, available at /redoc, shows documentation in a different style, focused on side navigation and greater emphasis on models.

Both interfaces can be useful depending on users' preferences.

The importance of documentation for the community and internal team lies in ensuring that developers understand what each endpoint does, what parameters are accepted, what return format to expect, and what errors can occur. An undocumented API creates confusion and rework. When the application evolves, teams need to update the doc. If this update is manual, gaps or omissions appear. By adopting automatic generation, each modification to the model or route is reflected in OpenAPI and, therefore, in the reading panel, eliminating inconsistencies.

Many teams use this feature to provide sandbox environments, where consumers can play with the API without resorting to external tools, discovering endpoints and testing payloads. In B2B integrations, adopting an interactive doc speeds up the learning curve and reduces support emails, as the partner team can see everything they need, test and adjust their requests directly in the Swagger interface. Routes that accept specific authentication or parameters can display fields for inserting tokens or credentials, demonstrating the correct way to send Authorization headers.

Several useful practices emerge to make the most of these functionalities. One of them is the use of tags, which categorize endpoints into groups, such as "items," "users," "auth," and "inventory." Each route can receive tags in its decorator, grouping them into sections in the interface:

python

```
# EXAMPLE 3
# STEP 1: grouping endpoints with tags
@app.get("/items", tags=["inventory"])
def list_items():
    return [{"name": "Pen", "price": 1.2}]
```

```python
@app.post("/items", tags=["inventory"])
def create_item(item: Item):
    return {"msg": "Item created"}
```

/docs or /redoc displays a tab for "inventory," listing these routes. On larger systems, this tagging scheme makes it easier to find endpoints related to specific resources. Another practice is to add docstrings or docstring parameters to the route definition, describing purposes, possible values and returns:

python

```python
# EXAMPLE 4
# STEP 1: docstring approach
@app.post("/login", tags=["auth"])
def login_user(
    username: str,
    password: str
):
    """
    Authenticates a user by username and password.
    Returns an access token that can be used for subsequent
requests.
    """
    # hypothetical logic
    return {"token": "abc123"}
```

The docstring is included in the endpoint description on the dashboard, helping consumers understand the context. Or you can use the decorator's summary and description parameters:

python

```python
# EXAMPLE 5
@app.post("/login", summary="User login",
```

```
description="Authenticates a user and returns a JWT token.")
def login_user(username: str, password: str):
    return {"token": "abc123"}
```

The summary appears as a title, and description provides additional details. The generated doc includes these texts, making it easier to read. When an endpoint has input parameters or returns templates, Pydantic classes define a schema that also appears in the doc, displaying each field, type, and constraint.

Another feature is to provide usage examples, so that the Swagger interface presents pre-populated examples. Each route or body parameter can have an examples. By clicking on these examples, the user loads the payload into the interface and executes the request, without having to type manually. This method reduces the likelihood of typing errors and provides clear instructions on how to format the request.

One way to demonstrate:

python

```
# EXAMPLE 6
# STEP 1: parameter with example
from fastapi import Body
from pydantic import BaseModel, Field

class Customer(BaseModel):
    name: str = Field(..., example="Alice")
    age: int = Field(..., example=30)

@app.post("/customers")
def create_customer(cust: Customer = Body(..., example={
    "name": "Bob",
    "age": 25
})):
    return {"created": cust.dict()}
```

In the interface, when expanding /customers, the body payload suggests name: "Bob" and age: 25. The name field, within the class, also has example "Alice," which appears in the schema. Thus, the doc combines all this information, displaying settings and formatting without requiring extra effort from the team. The route stays updated as class annotations or docstrings change.

Automatically generated documentation can be disabled or moved to another path if the application wishes to hide sensitive endpoints in production. On systems that don't want to expose /docs to the world, there are settings to change the route or require authentication. One approach is to provide the doc only in indoor or protected environments. The snippet:

python

```python
# EXAMPLE 7
# STEP 1: disable default docs
app = FastAPI(docs_url=None, redoc_url=None)

# if needed, define custom routes for documentation
@app.get("/docs-only-internally")
def internal_docs():
    # logic to serve the docs or redirect
    pass
```

This style allows you to control who sees the doc and when. In open source projects, it is customary to make it available as part of the service, helping the community to consume the API effortlessly. In corporate environments, the doc may reside behind a proxy or require administrators to log in.

Adopting a standardized doc style generates benefits for the entire community. Different teams that maintain independent microservices can employ the same doc format, defining conventions for tags, descriptions and templates. New developers get up to speed quickly. The end user of any route, be it a React front-end or a partner via B2B, does not need to dig through outdated wikis or PDFs, as the dashboard always reflects the current state of the code. If the application implements route versioning, it is also possible to define different roots or prefixes for v1, v2, and maintain a distinct doc for each version.

There is also the possibility of customizing the Swagger UI layout, adjusting colors and logos, or integrating with OAuth2 mechanisms. FastAPI uses the swagger-ui-bundle lib, which can be configured with extra parameters if the project wants a corporate look. In some scenarios, teams inject CSS or scripts to customize the experience. Recent framework updates allow replacing the native doc generator if someone prefers another interface. For most applications, the standard serves very well.

What is reflected in these resources is FastAPI's concern with simplifying maintenance and the adoption of good practices. Unlike solutions that rely on manually generated doc, any changes to routes, parameters, types, or models automatically propagate through the doc. The overhead of manual documentation and the chance of disagreements disappear. Python's typing and Pydantic's verification guarantee that what is displayed in Swagger is true, because if something is wrong, the framework itself refuses the request.

Best practices include grouping endpoints by functionality using coherent tags, inserting summaries and short descriptions of each route, specifying input and output models with Pydantic classes, and exemplifying typical uses. When the need arises to standardize nomenclature or status codes, the built-in doc displays it all. If the application sets 201 Created for a route, the doc indicates this status for the operation, eliminating confusion of "returns 200 or 201?" In the case of routes that throw custom exceptions with status 400, 404, or 409, you may want to explicitly document or use response_model and response codes, as OpenAPI enriches itself with this information.

An overview of the final doc might bring together login and logout routes under the "auth" tag, item creation routes under the "items" tag, and query routes under "inventory." The front-end team quickly navigates this organization and finds the desired route by inspecting the incoming and outgoing JSON. When you click the "Try it out" button, the interface loads an example JSON (if provided) and allows you to send the request to the server. The return appears in JSON format, with status code, headers and body. This makes development iterative and reduces friction between teams, as any payload discrepancies are identified before writing the front-end.

Another caution is that the doc does not replace good API design, because if the routes are poorly defined or the application does not follow HTTP standards, the doc will only reflect these poor choices. The advantage of FastAPI is that, by combining typing, Pydantic and automatic doc, the developer tends to think more carefully about each route and the data format. If each field requires explanation and the doc displays this format, the team notices inconsistencies or redundancies. This immediate feedback avoids chaotic evolutions, as any modification to the schema becomes visible.

There is also offline generation of the OpenAPI file, if the team wishes to export and use it in other tools. When accessing / openapi.json, the framework returns the JSON that describes the API. CI or offline doc tools can consume this file, generating PDFs, codegen clients, or static docs. It is feasible to integrate with scripts that convert this OpenAPI to other formats, sending the doc to dev portals or internal platforms. This way, local interactive doc and corporate offline doc needs stay in sync.

An additional recommendation is to include coherence in the naming of routes and fields in the design, because when the user examines /users, /items and /orders, they should notice a pattern. Routes like /users/{user_id}/orders and /users/{user_id}/profile exhibit consistency and make the doc clear. If the doc is generated but each route has confusing names or duplicate parameters, the advantage is lost. It is essential to minimally plan the structure so that the doc appears organized, with tags representing each resource or context, and summaries defining operations without repetitions. By doing this, the FastAPI doc reaches a professional level, looking like something that was created manually, but, in reality, it is the result of the systematic extraction of definitions from the code.

Many professionals say that the FastAPI doc is a crucial resource in adopting the framework, as it relieves the team of manual tasks, avoids mistakes and generates confidence for those who use the API. With automatic, interactive docs, the community grows quickly as new users learn the API in minutes and can launch proofs of concept without installing anything other than the browser. This viral effect favors integrations with front-ends, microservices and even QA teams, which use the doc to simulate test scenarios or load testing automations. In 2025 and beyond, the demand for speed and reliability is expected to increase, and FastAPI's automatic doc perfectly fits these requirements, uniting development and documentation in a single flow.

Some people customize swagger to insert branded links, legal disclaimers, or usage disclaimers. It is possible to include a swagger_custom_init.js file that adds extra scripts, or provide parameters when initializing FastAPI, adjusting swagger_ui_parameters and swagger_ui_init_oauth. This degree of customization meets the needs of companies that want to display logos or require OAuth2 integrated into the panel. The central point remains: the doc is generated from the routes and models, minimizing information gaps.

Adopting both interfaces (Swagger in /docs and Redoc in /redoc) is also common, as some teams prefer Redoc's usability, while others like Swagger's style. If you don't want one of the interfaces, you can disable it with docs_url or redoc_url parameters in the FastAPI constructor. In solutions that require specific dashboards, the dev can define custom routes and serve HTML that loads the Swagger UI or Redoc manually, indicating a remote JSON. The range of configurations appears to be very flexible.

In short, the automatic documentation in FastAPI revolves around the OpenAPI file generated by analyzing routes, HTTP methods, route and query parameters, as well as Pydantic classes that describe request bodies and responses. This built-in capability frees developers from writing separate specifications, synchronizes doc and deployment, speeds up new user onboarding, and makes it possible to test requests in the browser. Customizing the title, description, contact, tags and examples enriches the experience, transforming the doc into something pleasant and complete, even if the project is large. Achieving this result does not require complex configurations, as as soon as the project starts, /docs and /redoc are already available. With good naming practices and data structures, the final doc becomes a competitive differentiator, benefiting the community and support teams.

CHAPTER 16. INTEGRATION WITH DATABASES IN FASTAPI

Modern application development requires efficient integration with databases to store, retrieve and manipulate information reliably. In the context of FastAPI, the use of an ORM (Object-Relational Mapping) such as SQLAlchemy is highly recommended, as it facilitates the abstraction of interaction with the database, eliminating the need to write SQL queries directly. Additionally, using a migration tool like Alembic allows you to keep the database structure synchronized with the code, ensuring that changes to models are reflected without the need for manual changes.

The first step towards integrating FastAPI with databases involves configuring the connection, defining models and implementing CRUD (Create, Read, Update, Delete) operations. SQLAlchemy provides a powerful interface to manage tables, columns and relationships in a structured way, while FastAPI uses Pydantic capabilities to ensure that data received and returned by routes is always in the correct format.

Database configuration can be done by creating a connection engine and defining sessions to interact with the database. Below is a basic configuration example using SQLite:

python

```python
# EXAMPLE 1
# STEP 1: Configuring the database connection
from sqlalchemy import create_engine
from sqlalchemy.orm import sessionmaker
```

```python
DATABASE_URL = "sqlite:///./banco.db"

engine = create_engine(
    DATABASE_URL,
    connect_args={"check_same_thread": False} # Required for
SQLite in single-threaded environment
)
SessionLocal = sessionmaker(autocommit=False,
autoflush=False, bind=engine)
```

To connect to a PostgreSQL or MySQL database, simply modify the DATABASE_URL to the proper format, such as:

python

```python
DATABASE_URL = "postgresql://usuario:senha@localhost/
nome_do_banco"
```

Model definition in SQLAlchemy follows a structured pattern. Below is an example of modeling a table items:

python

```python
# EXAMPLE 2
# STEP 2: Defining SQLAlchemy models
from sqlalchemy import Column, Integer, String, Boolean,
Float
from sqlalchemy.ext.declarative import declarative_base

Base = declarative_base()

class Item(Base):
    __tablename__ = "items"

    id = Column(Integer, primary_key=True, index=True)
    name = Column(String, index=True)
    price = Column(Float)
```

```python
    description = Column(String, nullable=True)
    in_stock = Column(Boolean, default=True)
```

With the models defined, it is necessary to configure the database sessions within the FastAPI routes. To do this, we created a session manager to ensure that each request uses a separate connection:

python

```python
# EXAMPLE 3
# STEP 3: Database Session Manager
from fastapi import Depends
from sqlalchemy.orm import Session

def get_db():
    db = SessionLocal()
    try:
        yield db
    finally:
        db.close()
```

Now that the database is configured and the models have been created, it is possible to implement CRUD operations in the API routes. FastAPI facilitates this integration by using Pydantic to validate incoming and outgoing data. Below is an example route to create an item:

python

```python
# EXAMPLE 4
# STEP 4: Route to item creation
from fastapi import FastAPI, HTTPException
from pydantic import BaseModel

app = FastAPI()

class ItemSchema(BaseModel):
```

```
name: str
price: float
description: str | None = None

@app.post("/items/")
def create_item(item: ItemSchema, db: Session =
Depends(get_db)):
    db_item = Item(name=item.name, price=item.price,
description=item.description)
    db.add(db_item)
    db.commit()
    db.refresh(db_item)
    return db_item
```

The function create_item receives an object ItemSchema, automatically validates the data and inserts it into the database. The method commit() completes the transaction and refresh(db_item) reloads the data of the newly created item.

To search for an item by ID, the query can be done as follows:

python

```
# EXAMPLE 5
# STEP 5: Route to get item by ID
@app.get("/items/{item_id}")
def get_item(item_id: int, db: Session = Depends(get_db)):
    db_item = db.query(Item).filter(Item.id == item_id).first()
    if not db_item:
        raise HTTPException(status_code=404, detail="Item not
found")
    return db_item
```

If the requested item is not found, the function returns an HTTP 404 error.

Updating an item can be done with the following route:

python

```
# EXAMPLE 6
# STEP 6: Update an existing item
@app.put("/items/{item_id}")
def update_item(item_id: int, item_data: ItemSchema, db:
Session = Depends(get_db)):
    db_item = db.query(Item).filter(Item.id == item_id).first()
    if not db_item:
        raise HTTPException(status_code=404, detail="Item not
found")

    db_item.name = item_data.name
    db_item.price = item_data.price
    db_item.description = item_data.description
    db.commit()
    db.refresh(db_item)
    return db_item
```

The function update_item updates the item values in the database, ensuring that the change is reflected correctly.

To delete an item, the following route can be used:

python

```
# EXAMPLE 7
# STEP 7: Deleting an item
@app.delete("/items/{item_id}")
def delete_item(item_id: int, db: Session = Depends(get_db)):
    db_item = db.query(Item).filter(Item.id == item_id).first()
    if not db_item:
        raise HTTPException(status_code=404, detail="Item not
found")

    db.delete(db_item)
    db.commit()
    return {"msg": "Item deleted successfully"}
```

Migration Management with Alembic

When database models change, you need to synchronize these changes with the actual database structure. To do this, we use Alembic, which records and applies these changes automatically.

To start Alembic in a project, we run:

bash

```
album name album
```

This creates a directory structure where migration versions are stored. To configure correctly, you need to modify the file env.py, ensuring that it recognizes the models defined in the application.

Then, when making changes to a model, we generate a new migration with:

bash

```
alembic revision --autogenerate -m "Item model change"
```

And we apply the migration to the bank with:

bash

```
alembic upgrade head
```

This process ensures that any new developer or environment can recreate the database structure without errors.

FastAPI's integration with databases using SQLAlchemy and Alembic offers a complete solution for data manipulation in modern applications. The use of ORM makes it easier to create and maintain tables, while FastAPI, combined with Pydantic, ensures that data received and returned is always structured correctly. The inclusion of migration tools like Alembic simplifies database evolution without the need for direct manual changes.

By following this development flow, it is possible to create robust, scalable and secure APIs, taking advantage of the best of technology for data manipulation. The use of good practices such as separation of responsibilities, clear definition of models and well-structured routes contributes to the construction of efficient and easy-to-maintain systems, ensuring a high standard of quality in software development.

CHAPTER 17. AUTHENTICATION AND SECURITY IN FASTAPI

Creating secure APIs is one of the pillars for developing reliable systems. In modern projects, implementing robust authentication and access control mechanisms becomes essential to protect sensitive data and prevent unauthorized users from accessing critical resources. FastAPI, combined with specialized libraries, offers complete support for the implementation of authentication systems using standards such as JWT and OAuth2, in addition to allowing efficient management of tokens and sessions. Below is a detailed approach to configuring and implementing these features, accompanied by code snippets, practical examples, and security tips that ensure an API prepared for the market challenges of 2025.

The process begins by defining the basis for authentication. In many cases, the strategy adopted involves the use of JWT tokens to identify users and ensure that each request is accompanied by a valid credential. To do this, you need to install libraries that facilitate the creation, signing and verification of tokens. For example, the PyJWT library allows the manipulation of JSON Web Tokens in a simple way, easily integrating with FastAPI. When defining a login route, the credentials provided by the user are checked and, if valid, a token is generated containing essential information, such as the user ID and role, which will be useful for access control later.

Below is an illustrative excerpt for generating a JWT token, using PyJWT:

python

```python
# Code for generating JWT token
import jwt
from datetime import datetime, timedelta

SECRET_KEY = "a_supersecret_key" # This key must be strong
and kept in a secure environment
ALGORITHM = "HS256"
ACCESS_TOKEN_EXPIRE_MINUTES = 30

def create_access_token(data: dict) -> str:
    to_encode = data.copy()
    expire = datetime.utcnow() +
timedelta(minutes=ACCESS_TOKEN_EXPIRE_MINUTES)
    to_encode.update({"exp": expire})
    token = jwt.encode(to_encode, SECRET_KEY,
algorithm=ALGORITHM)
    return token
```

In the login route, credentials are checked; if they are correct, the above function generates a token that is returned to the client. This token must be included in all subsequent requests, normally in the Authorization header as Bearer token. As an example, the login route can be defined as follows:

python

```python
# Code for login route with JWT
from fastapi import FastAPI, HTTPException, Depends
from pydantic import BaseModel

app = FastAPI()

class LoginData(BaseModel):
    username: str
    password: str
```

```python
# Hypothetical function that validates username and
password
def authenticate_user(username: str, password: str) -> dict |
None:
    # Authentication logic must check the database or other
repository
    if username == "admin" and password == "password":
        return {"user_id": 1, "role": "admin"}
    return None

@app.post("/login")
def login(data: LoginData):
    user = authenticate_user(data.username, data.password)
    if not user:
        raise HTTPException(status_code=401, detail="Invalid
credentials")
    token = create_access_token({"user_id": user["user_id"],
"role": user["role"]})
    return {"access_token": token, "token_type": "bearer"}
```

When logging in, the client receives a token that must be used in protected requests. From that point forward, each route that requires authentication can be protected with dependencies that validate the presence and veracity of the token. FastAPI allows you to define a dependency function that extracts the token from the header and decodes it to retrieve user data. The following is a token extraction and verification function:

python

```python
# Code for JWT token verification dependency
from fastapi import Security, HTTPException, status
from fastapi.security import HTTPBearer,
HTTPAuthorizationCredentials

security = HTTPBearer()
```

```
def get_current_user(token: HTTPAuthorizationCredentials =
Security(security)) -> dict:
    try:
        payload = jwt.decode(token.credentials, SECRET_KEY,
algorithms=[ALGORITHM])
        return payload # The payload must contain information
such as user_id and role
    except jwt.PyJWTError:
        raise
HTTPException(status_code=status.HTTP_401_UNAUTHORI
ZED, detail="Token inválido ou expirado")
```

Protected routes can then use this dependency to ensure that the user is authenticated. For example, a route that returns sensitive data might be defined like this:

python

```
# Code for protected route using JWT token
@app.get("/protected")
def protected_route(current_user: dict =
Depends(get_current_user)):
    return {"message": f"Hello, user {current_user['user_id']}
with role {current_user['role']}."}
```

In addition to JWT, OAuth2 is a widely used standard for access delegation. FastAPI has native support for OAuth2 with Password Flow, allowing the API to integrate with identity providers or offer its own authentication infrastructure. In the password flow, the client submits their credentials and, if valid, receives a token. In an OAuth2 implementation, the dependencies provided by FastAPI help to build the flow with few lines of code.

An example configuration with OAuth2 Password Flow using the Bearer schema can be structured as follows:

python

```
# Code for configuring OAuth2 with Password Flow
from fastapi.security import OAuth2PasswordBearer,
OAuth2PasswordRequestForm

oauth2_scheme = OAuth2PasswordBearer(tokenUrl="/token")

@app.post("/token")
def login_for_access_token(form_data:
OAuth2PasswordRequestForm = Depends()):
    user = authenticate_user(form_data.username,
form_data.password)
    if not user:
        raise HTTPException(status_code=401, detail="Invalid
credentials")
    token = create_access_token({"user_id": user["user_id"],
"role": user["role"]})
    return {"access_token": token, "token_type": "bearer"}
```

In the flow above, the /token route is the point where the client sends credentials via form data. OAuth2PasswordBearer defines a security scheme that extracts the token from subsequent requests, working in a similar way to the HTTPBearer shown previously. This integration with OAuth2 makes the system flexible for a variety of needs, including integration with external providers or internal implementation of strong authentication.

Token and session management is crucial to maintaining a consistent user experience. In addition to generating tokens to identify users, it is important to implement renewal and revocation strategies. The JWT token, by nature, is self-contained and has a defined expiration time. Once expired, the user needs to log in again or use a refresh token mechanism, which grants a new access token without the need to repeat the entire authentication process.

Managing refresh tokens involves creating a separate flow that securely stores a refresh token associated with the user. This token has a longer validity and, when sent together with the expired token, allows the issuance of a new access token. The implementation can use the same token generation mechanism, but with different expiration times. It is essential that refresh tokens are stored in a secure repository, possibly in a database, and that their use is limited to specific operations. For example, the refresh route can be constructed like this:

python

```python
# Code for managing refresh tokens
REFRESH_TOKEN_EXPIRE_DAYS = 7

def create_refresh_token(data: dict) -> str:
    to_encode = data.copy()
    expire = datetime.utcnow() +
timedelta(days=REFRESH_TOKEN_EXPIRE_DAYS)
    to_encode.update({"exp": expire})
    return jwt.encode(to_encode, SECRET_KEY,
algorithm=ALGORITHM)

@app.post("/refresh")
def refresh_token(refresh_token: str):
    try:
        payload = jwt.decode(refresh_token, SECRET_KEY,
algorithms=[ALGORITHM])
        new_token = create_access_token({"user_id":
payload["user_id"], "role": payload["role"]})
        return {"access_token": new_token, "token_type":
"bearer"}
    except jwt.PyJWTError:
        raise HTTPException(status_code=401, detail="Refresh
token invalid")
```

The token renewal flow allows when the access token expires, the client sends the refresh token to obtain a new, valid token. This process must be secure, with tokens revoked when the user logs out or changes their credentials. Additionally, token management can include activity logging to identify suspicious uses and prevent compromised tokens from being used for improper access.

Access and permissions control is based on determining what each user can or cannot access based on their role or group membership. By using the decoded token, the system can check the "role" value or other information contained in the payload to define the authorization of each route. A simple mechanism involves creating a dependent function that checks whether the user has the necessary permission to perform an action. A snippet of code exemplifies this approach:

python

```python
# Code for role-based access control
def require_role(required_role: str):
    def role_checker(current_user: dict =
Depends(get_current_user)):
        if current_user.get("role") != required_role:
            raise HTTPException(status_code=403,
detail="Access denied")
        return current_user
    return role_checker

@app.get("/admin")
def admin_area(current_user: dict =
Depends(require_role("admin"))):
    return {"message": f"Welcome, administrator
{current_user.get('user_id')}"}
```

The require_role function takes the required role and returns a function that, when used as a dependency, ensures that the token contains the correct role. If the user does not have permission, the system responds with HTTP 403 Forbidden, blocking access to sensitive resources. This approach can be expanded to accept multiple roles by checking whether the user's role is on a list of valid permissions. This flexibility is crucial for systems with complex hierarchies, where different access levels determine which endpoints can be accessed.

Security strategies for APIs involve several layers of protection that go beyond basic authentication. The implementation of HTTPS is essential to protect data transmission, preventing tokens or credentials from being intercepted by malicious agents. Configuring the server to use TLS, forcing the use of valid certificates, and setting security headers such as Strict-Transport-Security help reduce risk. In conjunction with this, it is essential to set session cookies with Secure and HttpOnly flags, ensuring that sensitive information cannot be accessed by client-side scripts or transmitted over unencrypted connections.

Preventing Cross-Site Request Forgery (CSRF) attacks is another important concern. Although the JWT approach reduces some vulnerabilities associated with CSRF, when the application uses cookies to store tokens, it is necessary to include verification mechanisms. The use of CSRF tokens, generated and verified by the server, prevents malicious requests from being executed on the user's behalf. Integration with libraries that take care of this aspect, or manually implementing a verification system, makes the API more resistant to these types of attacks.

Protection against code injection and SQL Injection is guaranteed when using ORMs and parameterized queries. Using SQLAlchemy, for example, prevents user-submitted data from being interpreted as part of an SQL query, since the parameters are handled securely. Additionally, validating and sanitizing inputs using Pydantic models and custom validators ensures that malicious data does not penetrate the system.

Another layer of security involves rate limiting and protection against denial of service (DDoS) attacks. Configuring rate limiting policies prevents a single IP from making excessive requests, forcing the API to deny or delay requests that exceed the established limit. Tools and middleware can be integrated into the application to monitor the number of requests, recording and blocking suspicious patterns. The use of distributed caching solutions, such as Redis, in conjunction with token bucket or leaky bucket algorithms, makes it possible to implement these policies in a scalable way.

Monitoring API activity with logs and alerts is critical to security. Integrating the system with monitoring platforms, which alert to abnormal access patterns, authentication failures or prohibited access attempts, increases the ability to respond to incidents. A robust log, which records the requester's IP, the route accessed, the time and status of the response, helps to quickly identify vulnerable points and act preventively. Configuring log levels (DEBUG, INFO, WARNING, ERROR, CRITICAL) and directing logs to a centralized system improves visibility and incident management.

Adopting continuous dependency update and review practices is also part of a security strategy. Keeping libraries up to date ensures that known vulnerabilities are fixed, while regularly auditing code and applying security tests (such as SAST and DAST) identify flaws before they can be exploited. Checking the integrity of the environment, reviewing firewall configurations and network segmentation are measures that, although external to the code, complement API security.

An interesting approach is implementing multi-factor

authentication (MFA) for sensitive operations. In systems where security is critical, in addition to the password, the user may be asked to provide a temporary code generated by an application or sent via SMS. This extra layer of verification significantly reduces the risk of unauthorized access, even if the password is compromised. Integration with libraries that support TOTP (Time-based One-Time Password) or SMS solutions allows you to add this requirement with relative ease.

Another important strategy is the use of security headers and content policies (Content Security Policy, CSP). Configuring the server to send headers that prevent XSS (Cross-Site Scripting) attacks and content injection helps shield the application against attacks that exploit the manipulation of content displayed in the browser. Headers such as X-Content-Type-Options, X-Frame-Options and X-XSS-Protection are configurable at the server level or via middleware and should always be applied in production environments.

The integration of forced logout and session management mechanisms is essential to ensure that, at the end of the interaction or in cases of suspected compromise, sessions are closed securely. Logout routes that invalidate tokens, remove cookies, and record the action in the security log allow the system to maintain tight control over who is accessing resources. Token revocation, especially in systems that use JWT, can be implemented through a revoked token repository or through a mechanism that invalidates old tokens when updating the user's password.

A practical implementation for logout and session revocation can be developed by integrating a database or cache to record inactive tokens, so that if a token is used after being marked as revoked, access is automatically blocked. This strategy is useful in corporate environments, where data security is a priority and any improper access can have serious consequences.

Protecting routes through dependencies that verify user authenticity and permissions, using token verification and role checking functions, consolidates the security strategy. By defining functions that validate whether the user has the level of access necessary for a given operation, the API becomes more resilient to authorization failures. This logic can be implemented in dependency form, using FastAPI's Depends feature, which injects the check before executing the route. An example function for checking permissions can be constructed as follows:

python

```
# Code for checking access permission
from fastapi import Depends, HTTPException, status

def require_role(required_role: str):
    def role_checker(current_user: dict =
Depends(get_current_user)):
        if current_user.get("role") != required_role:
            raise
HTTPException(status_code=status.HTTP_403_FORBIDDEN,
detail="Acesso negado")
        return current_user
    return role_checker

@app.get("/dashboard")
def dashboard(current_user: dict =
Depends(require_role("admin"))):
    return {"message": f"Welcome to the dashboard, user
{current_user.get('user_id')}"}
```

This dependency ensures that only users with the "admin" role can access the /dashboard route. If the user's token does not have this information, the request is blocked, reinforcing access control.

To protect the API against denial of service (DDoS) attacks, implementing rate limiting and caching policies is essential. Using middleware or external services that monitor the frequency of requests by IP can prevent malicious users from overloading the system. Configuring limits, such as the maximum number of requests per minute, and applying caching techniques for static responses, contribute to keeping the API responsive even under high demand.

Another critical aspect involves the configuration of CORS (Cross-Origin Resource Sharing). If the API is consumed by web applications hosted on different domains, it is necessary to define which origins are allowed to access the resources. Configuring CORS headers correctly prevents unwanted requests from being made from unauthorized websites, increasing the overall security of the system. FastAPI offers a middleware for CORS that can be configured as follows:

python

```
# CORS configuration in FastAPI
from fastapi.middleware.cors import CORSMiddleware

app.add_middleware(
    CORSMiddleware,
    allow_origins=["https://www.seudominio.com"],
    allow_credentials=True,
    allow_methods=["*"],
    allow_headers=["*"],
)
```

By restricting the permitted origins, the system ensures that only the authorized domain can interact with the API, reducing the risk of attacks via browsers.

In environments where security is a priority, the use of HSTS

(HTTP Strict Transport Security) and the mandatory HTTPS for all requests ensure that the data transmitted is always encrypted. Configuring these policies on the web server or directly in the application prevents sensitive information from being intercepted or modified during transmission.

Integration with monitoring and auditing systems is also vital for security. Recording each access attempt, whether successful or not, allows staff to identify suspicious patterns of behavior and quickly react to incidents. Detailed logs, which include information such as IP, user agent, route accessed and response time, can be sent to SIEM (Security Information and Event Management) systems for continuous analysis. This practice helps prevent attacks and maintain system integrity.

Additional measures, such as implementing multi-factor authentication (MFA), raise the level of protection even further. In applications that deal with highly sensitive data, requiring the user to provide a temporary code, generated by an authenticator application or sent via SMS, in addition to the password, adds an extra layer of security. Integrating FastAPI with libraries that support TOTP (Time-based One-Time Password) allows the creation of hassle-free MFA flows, reinforcing trust in users' identity.

Another important aspect is token management. In systems that use JWT, tokens have a built-in expiration time. It is recommended to implement a token renewal route, where the user sends an expired or about-to-expire token and receives a new one, without having to go through the entire login process again. This strategy improves user experience and maintains security by allowing you to revoke old tokens when necessary, such as in cases of password change or suspected compromise.

Token revocation can be managed by keeping a record of invalidated tokens in a database or cache. When a request arrives, the system checks whether the token is still valid or has been revoked, blocking access otherwise. This mechanism is especially important in corporate environments, where security must be maintained even after credentials are revoked. A simple approach involves creating a table of revoked tokens and querying this table on each authenticated request.

Using dependencies to inject security logic into each route makes the code more modular and testable. By centralizing validation and permissions checking into reusable functions, the application reduces code duplication and facilitates future security policy updates. Furthermore, the configuration of middleware that monitors and limits requests, adjusts headers and forces secure connections completes the set of strategies to protect the API against different types of attacks.

To summarize, integrating authentication and security in FastAPI requires implementing robust authentication systems, using standards such as JWT and OAuth2, in addition to managing tokens and sessions securely. Access control based on roles and permissions, combined with protection strategies such as HTTPS, CORS, rate limiting and continuous monitoring, builds an API that is resilient against attacks and vulnerabilities. Each piece of code and each dependency must be configured to maintain data integrity and user trust.

The following is a comprehensive example that demonstrates the complete implementation of authentication, token management, access control, and application of security strategies:

python

```
# Complete code integrating authentication with JWT, access control and security
import jwt
from datetime import datetime, timedelta
from fastapi import FastAPI, HTTPException, Depends, status, Security
```

```python
from fastapi.security import OAuth2PasswordBearer,
OAuth2PasswordRequestForm, HTTPBearer,
HTTPAuthorizationCredentials
from pydantic import BaseModel, EmailStr
from typing import Optional

# Basic settings
SECRET_KEY = "a_supersecret_key_for_the_project"
ALGORITHM = "HS256"
ACCESS_TOKEN_EXPIRE_MINUTES = 30
REFRESH_TOKEN_EXPIRE_DAYS = 7

app = FastAPI(
    title="Secure API with FastAPI",
    description="API that demonstrates authentication, access
control and security strategies using FastAPI",
    version="1.0.0"
)

# Pydantic models for data input and output
class User(BaseModel):
    user_id: int
    username: str
    email: EmailStr
    role: str

class Token(BaseModel):
    access_token: str
    token_type: str

class LoginData(BaseModel):
    username: str
    password: str

# Helper functions for creating tokens
def create_access_token(data: dict) -> str:
    to_encode = data.copy()
```

```python
    expire = datetime.utcnow() +
timedelta(minutes=ACCESS_TOKEN_EXPIRE_MINUTES)
    to_encode.update({"exp": expire})
    return jwt.encode(to_encode, SECRET_KEY,
algorithm=ALGORITHM)

def create_refresh_token(data: dict) -> str:
    to_encode = data.copy()
    expire = datetime.utcnow() +
timedelta(days=REFRESH_TOKEN_EXPIRE_DAYS)
    to_encode.update({"exp": expire})
    return jwt.encode(to_encode, SECRET_KEY,
algorithm=ALGORITHM)

# Simulated authentication function
def authenticate_user(username: str, password: str) ->
Optional[dict]:
    # Simulation: admin user with password 'password'
    if username == "admin" and password == "password":
        return {"user_id": 1, "username": "admin", "email":
"admin@example.com", "role": "admin"}
    if username == "user" and password == "password":
        return {"user_id": 2, "username": "user", "email":
"user@example.com", "role": "user"}
    return None

# OAuth2 configuration for token extraction
oauth2_scheme = OAuth2PasswordBearer(tokenUrl="/token")
http_bearer = HTTPBearer()

# Dependency to get current user from token
def get_current_user(token: HTTPAuthorizationCredentials =
Security(http_bearer)) -> dict:
    try:
        payload = jwt.decode(token.credentials, SECRET_KEY,
algorithms=[ALGORITHM])
        return payload
```

```python
    except jwt.PyJWTError:
        raise
HTTPException(status_code=status.HTTP_401_UNAUTHORI
ZED, detail="Token inválido ou expirado")

# Route to login with OAuth2 Password Flow
@app.post("/token", response_model=Token,
tags=["Authentication"])
def login_for_access_token(form_data:
OAuth2PasswordRequestForm = Depends()):
    user = authenticate_user(form_data.username,
form_data.password)
    if not user:
        raise HTTPException(status_code=401, detail="Invalid
credentials")
    access_token = create_access_token({"user_id":
user["user_id"], "role": user["role"]})
    refresh_token = create_refresh_token({"user_id":
user["user_id"], "role": user["role"]})
    return {"access_token": access_token, "token_type":
"bearer"}

# Route for token renewal
@app.post("/refresh", response_model=Token,
tags=["Authentication"])
def refresh_access_token(refresh_token: str):
    try:
        payload = jwt.decode(refresh_token, SECRET_KEY,
algorithms=[ALGORITHM])
        new_access_token = create_access_token({"user_id":
payload["user_id"], "role": payload["role"]})
        return {"access_token": new_access_token, "token_type":
"bearer"}
    except jwt.PyJWTError:
        raise HTTPException(status_code=401, detail="Refresh
token inválido")
```

```python
# Function for checking permission based on user role
def require_role(required_role: str):
    def role_checker(current_user: dict =
Depends(get_current_user)):
        if current_user.get("role") != required_role:
            raise HTTPException(status_code=403,
detail="Access denied")
        return current_user
    return role_checker

# Example route protected by authentication
@app.get("/protected", tags=["Security"])
def protected_route(current_user: dict =
Depends(get_current_user)):
    return {"message": f"Hello, user {current_user['user_id']}
with role {current_user['role']}"}

# Restricted route for administrators
@app.get("/admin", tags=["Security"])
def admin_area(current_user: dict =
Depends(require_role("admin"))):
    return {"message": f"Welcome, administrator
{current_user['user_id']}"}

# Route for simulated logout (on systems with JWT tokens,
logout is usually managed on the client or with token
revocation)
@app.post("/logout", tags=["Authentication"])
def logout(current_user: dict = Depends(get_current_user)):
    # In real implementations, the token can be added to a
revocation list
    return {"message": "Logout successfully"}

# Example of protected route with access limitation and
verification of CORS, HTTPS and security headers
@app.get("/secure-data", tags=["Security"])
```

```python
def get_secure_data(current_user: dict =
Depends(get_current_user)):
    return {"data": "Sensitive information available only to
authenticated users"}

# Implementation of middleware for request logging, useful
for auditing and monitoring
@app.middleware("http")
async def log_requests(request, call_next):
    # Simple registration: access path and time
    print(f"Request for {request.url.path} at
{datetime.utcnow().isoformat()}")
    response = await call_next(request)
    print(f"Resposta com status {response.status_code} para
{request.url.path}")
    return response

# CORS settings to restrict allowed origins
from fastapi.middleware.cors import CORSMiddleware

app.add_middleware(
    CORSMiddleware,
    allow_origins=["https://www.yourdomain.com"],
    allow_credentials=True,
    allow_methods=["*"],
    allow_headers=["*"]
)

# Additional protection with security headers can be
configured on the web server or via custom middleware
@app.middleware("http")
async def add_security_headers(request, call_next):
    response = await call_next(request)
    response.headers["X-Content-Type-Options"] = "nosniff"
    response.headers["X-Frame-Options"] = "DENY"
    response.headers["X-XSS-Protection"] = "1; mode=block"
    return response
```

```
# Example of protection against brute force attacks, limiting
the number of requests (the logic can be integrated with Redis
or another caching system)
from fastapi_limiter import FastAPILimiter
from fastapi_limiter.depends import RateLimiter
import redis.asyncio as redis

@app.on_event("startup")
async def startup():
    redis_client = redis.Redis(host="localhost", port=6379,
db=0, encoding="utf-8", decode_responses=True)
    await FastAPILimiter.init(redis_client)

@app.get("/limited",
dependencies=[Depends(RateLimiter(times=5, seconds=60))],
tags=["Segurança"])
def limited_endpoint():
    return {"message": "You have not exceeded the request
limit."}

# Monitoring and auditing strategies may include integration
with external services
@app.get("/audit", tags=["Auditoria"])
def audit_logs(current_user: dict =
Depends(get_current_user)):
    # This route simulates returning access logs for the current
user; in production, the logs would be in a centralized system
    return {"logs": f"Access logs for user
{current_user['user_id']}"}

# Route for MFA (Multi-Factor Authentication) simulation
from random import randint

@app.post("/mfa", tags=["Authentication"])
def mfa_challenge(username: str):
    # Generates a temporary code for multi-factor
```

authentication and simulates sending it via SMS or app

```
mfa_code = randint(100000, 999999)
# In a real system, the code would be sent via SMS or email
return {"message": f"MFA code generated for {username}",
"mfa_code": mfa_code}
```

Implementing authentication and security with FastAPI combines the robustness of JWT and OAuth2 with advanced access control and threat protection strategies. The use of middleware for logging, the application of security headers, the configuration of CORS and rate limiting, in addition to the management of tokens and sessions, form a complete ecosystem that protects the API against different types of attacks. The adoption of MFA and the possibility of integration with external audit systems further raise the level of security, preparing the application for the challenges of the current digital environment. The presented architecture allows developers to create secure endpoints, with validated and protected responses, ensuring that each request is monitored, authenticated and authorized in a transparent way. This integrated approach not only increases reliability and performance, but also promotes an agile development flow aligned with industry best practices, making the API a reliable and resilient component within any service ecosystem.

By centralizing security strategies, teams can focus on developing features without worrying about data integrity, knowing that each layer of the system is designed to resist attacks and minimize risks. The documentation automatically generated by FastAPI, combined with the implementation of dependencies for checking tokens and permissions, provides a clear picture of how resources are protected. This way, both API developers and consumers benefit from an environment where information is secure, operations are audited, and the user experience remains consistent and reliable.

The combination of robust authentication, token management, permissions verification and the implementation of security policies, such as HTTPS, CORS and rate limiting, creates an infrastructure prepared to serve everything from simple applications to mission-critical systems. Using JWT and OAuth2 ensures interoperability with other services and facilitates integration with external identity providers. The modularization of the code, with the use of dependencies and middleware, makes the system highly testable and easy to maintain, allowing updates and improvements to be implemented without significant risks of breaking functionality.

Constant monitoring, both of access and attack attempts, is essential to quickly identify and respond to security incidents. Integrating the API with SIEM tools and using detailed logs helps in detecting abnormal patterns and taking preventive measures. This proactive approach, combined with the implementation of multi-factor authentication strategies, ensures that the application is always one step ahead of potential threats.

The ability to refresh tokens and revoke compromised sessions protects system integrity even in partial hack scenarios. The use of refresh routes, combined with careful management of refresh tokens and a strict token expiration policy, prevents old credentials from remaining active for long periods, reducing the risk of unauthorized access. Every aspect of token management is carefully integrated into the authentication flow, providing an environment where access renewal happens transparently, without compromising data security.

Finally, the integration of authentication and security in FastAPI demonstrates that a well-architected system can

CHAPTER 18. DEPLOY AND SCALABILITY OF APPLICATIONS WITH FASTAPI

Preparing an application for production requires care that goes far beyond simply writing the code. In a development environment, the main focus is to implement features and perform tests; In production, attention turns to safety, performance, reliability and ease of maintenance. For applications built with FastAPI, these needs are met through adequate environment configuration, use of robust ASGI servers, flexible deployment strategies and constant performance monitoring. Each step must be carefully planned so that the application can scale efficiently and adapt to access peaks without losing service quality.

To begin with, preparing the application for production involves configuring essential environment variables, defining appropriate logs, ensuring that the application operates in production mode (by disabling debugging), and applying security policies such as HTTPS. Using a separate configuration file, where sensitive information such as secret keys and database connection strings are stored securely, is essential. Furthermore, the application must be packaged in such a way that the source code and static resources are organized, facilitating future updates and deployment in different environments.

A configuration file can be structured using libraries like python-dotenv to load environment variables from an .env file. An example configuration would be:

python

```python
# config.py
import them
from dotenv import load_dotenv

load_dotenv()

SECRET_KEY = os.getenv("SECRET_KEY")
DATABASE_URL = os.getenv("DATABASE_URL")
ENVIRONMENT = os.getenv("ENVIRONMENT", "production")
```

This practice ensures that sensitive data is not hard-coded and can be easily changed without modifying the main repository.

Using ASGI servers (uvicorn, hypercorn) is the next step to ensure that the application runs with high performance and scalability. FastAPI is built on the ASGI standard, which makes it possible to create asynchronous applications capable of handling multiple requests efficiently. Uvicorn is a lightweight and fast ASGI server, while Hypercorn offers additional features such as HTTP/2 support. The choice between one and the other depends on the specific requirements of the project. Uvicorn is often used due to its simplicity and excellent performance in high-concurrency scenarios.

Configuring uvicorn for production involves setting parameters such as number of workers, timeout and SSL usage. A typical command to start the server in production with uvicorn might be:

bash

```bash
uvicorn main:app --host 0.0.0.0 --port 8000 --workers 4 --timeout-keep-alive 75 --ssl-keyfile=/path/to/key.pem --ssl-certfile=/path/to/cert.pem
```

This configuration distributes the load between 4 workers,

keeping connections active for up to 75 seconds, and forces the use of HTTPS with SSL certificates. For environments that demand high availability, the use of Hypercorn can be considered, changing only the startup command:

bash

```
hypercorn main:app --bind 0.0.0.0:8000 --workers 4 --keep-alive 75 --keyfile /path/to/key.pem --certfile /path/to/cert.pem
```

These options ensure that the application is prepared to handle large volumes of requests, avoiding bottlenecks and improving the user experience.

Deployment strategies encompass several approaches, from creating Docker containers to using cloud services and orchestrating with Kubernetes. Docker is widely used to package the application, ensuring that it runs identically in any environment, regardless of operating system configurations or installed dependencies. A typical Dockerfile for a FastAPI application can be written as follows:

dockerfile

```
# EXAMPLE 1
FROM python:3.10-slim

ENV PYTHONDONTWRITEBYTECODE 1
ENV PYTHONUNBUFFERED 1

WORKDIR /app

COPY requirements.txt /app/
RUN pip install --upgrade pip && pip install -r requirements.txt

COPY . /app/
```

```
CMD ["uvicorn", "main:app", "--host", "0.0.0.0", "--port", "8000"]
```

This Dockerfile defines an image based on Python 3.10-slim, copies the requirements file and the rest of the code, installing the dependencies and starting the uvicorn server. In a production environment, it is recommended to use optimized images, minimizing size and eliminating unnecessary development tools.

The use of orchestrators such as Kubernetes allows the application to be scaled horizontally, distributed across multiple nodes and managed in a resilient way. Configuring a Kubernetes deployment involves defining YAML files that describe the pods, services, volumes, and scaling policies. A basic deployment for a FastAPI application can be structured like this:

yaml

```yaml
# deployment.yaml
apiVersion: apps/v1
kind: Deployment
metadata:
  name: fastapi-deployment
  labels:
    app: fastapi
spec:
  replicas: 3
  selector:
    matchLabels:
      app: fastapi
  template:
    metadata:
      labels:
        app: fastapi
    spec:
```

```
containers:
  - name: fastapi-container
    image: your_image_docker:latest
    ports:
     - containerPort: 8000
    resources:
     requests:
       cpu: "250m"
       memory: "256Mi"
     limits:
       cpu: "500m"
       memory: "512Mi"
    env:
     - name: SECRET_KEY
      valueFrom:
        secretKeyRef:
          name: fastapi-secrets
          key: secret_key
```

This deployment creates 3 replicas of the application, ensuring that if one instance fails, others will take over the load. Resource configurations and environment variables are defined to maintain consistency and security. The associated Kubernetes service exposes the application outside the cluster, and autoscaling policies can be configured to adjust the number of replicas based on load.

Another deployment strategy involves cloud platforms such as AWS, Google Cloud or Azure. These platforms offer managed services for containers, such as AWS Fargate or Google Cloud Run, that abstract the underlying infrastructure and facilitate autoscaling. For example, using AWS Fargate, the application runs in containers without the need to manage servers, and scaling is done according to demand, without manual intervention. Services such as AWS Elastic Beanstalk can also be configured to host the FastAPI application, integrating with load balancers, monitoring and logs.

Monitoring and scalability are key to keeping the application healthy and responsive. Tools like Prometheus and Grafana can be integrated to collect real-time metrics such as CPU usage, memory, request latency, number of active connections and error rate. Custom middleware can be added to the application to record these metrics or use existing libraries to integrate with Prometheus. An example of how to expose metrics in a FastAPI application could be:

python

```
# EXAMPLE 2
from fastapi import FastAPI
from prometheus_fastapi_instrumentator import
Instrumentator

app = FastAPI()
Instrumentator().instrument(app).expose(app)
```

This simple integration exposes metrics in the /metrics route, which can be collected by a Prometheus server for visualization in a Grafana dashboard. Analyzing these metrics helps you identify bottlenecks, adjust scaling settings, and plan resources to meet access spikes.

Horizontal scalability is guaranteed when running multiple replicas of the application, as demonstrated in deployments with Kubernetes or cloud container services. Additionally, techniques such as response caching using Redis or Memcached can be implemented to reduce the load on parts of the application that do not change frequently, such as heavy query results or static information. Configuring a distributed cache improves latency and performance, especially in high-volume scenarios. Integrating FastAPI with Redis is simple, using libraries like aioredis for asynchronous operations:

python

```
# EXAMPLE 3
import aioredis
from fastapi import FastAPI

app = FastAPI()

@app.on_event("startup")
async def startup():
    app.state.redis = await aioredis.from_url("redis://
localhost:6379", decode_responses=True)

@app.on_event("shutdown")
async def shutdown():
    await app.state.redis.close()

@app.get("/cache")
async def get_cached_data():
    value = await app.state.redis.get("key")
    if not value:
        value = "updated data"
        await app.state.redis.set("key", value, ex=60) # Expires in
60 seconds
    return {"value": value}
```

In this flow, when starting the application, Redis is connected and stored in the app.state object. The /cache route attempts to retrieve a value; if not found, defines a new value and configures the expiration time. This technique reduces the need to make repetitive calls to expensive operations such as database queries.

Ensuring that the application is prepared for a high-demand environment also involves the use of load balancers and autoscaling systems. On traditional servers, a load balancer distributes requests among multiple application instances, ensuring that no instance is overloaded. In cloud environments, autoscaling services monitor metrics and automatically adjust the number of active instances, avoiding downtime and improving the user experience. Correctly configuring these systems requires knowledge of API access patterns and available resources, but the advantages in terms of performance and resilience are significant.

Furthermore, it is essential to package the application in such a way that dependencies are managed and the environment is replicable. Using tools like Docker and Docker Compose allows you to create immutable images that can run in any compatible environment. A well-written Dockerfile, as presented previously, simplifies deployment and ensures that the application is always running with the same library versions and configurations, regardless of the production environment. This consistency prevents surprises and reduces the likelihood of failures due to divergences between development and production.

For teams operating in more complex environments, integrating the application with CI/CD (Continuous Integration/Continuous Deployment) tools is essential. Automated deployment pipelines ensure that, with each commit, the application is tested, packaged and deployed in staging or production environments. These pipelines can include build steps, unit testing, security verification, and running database migrations. A well-structured CI/CD flow reduces deployment time and increases system reliability, as each step is monitored and validated.

Application scalability can be maximized using engineering practices that aim to optimize code, minimize redundant calls and use asynchronous techniques for I/O operations. Although FastAPI is already designed to take advantage of the ASGI standard and run asynchronously, the design of routes and the correct use of dependencies also influence overall performance. Improving the efficiency of database queries, for example, can reduce latency and load on application instances. Furthermore, configuring cache usage, optimizing internal logic and distributing tasks into processing queues (such as using Celery) help the application remain responsive even under high demand.

Integration with monitoring tools allows you to detect points of failure and make proactive adjustments. Using Prometheus to collect metrics and Grafana to visualize graphs of CPU usage, memory, latency, and error rate provides valuable information for the team. When the system experiences spikes in access, the team can adjust the number of workers, increase resource capacity or even identify which endpoint needs to be optimized. This iterative approach to monitoring and tuning ensures that the application remains stable even as the volume of requests grows.

The adoption of security practices when deploying is also necessary. Using HTTPS is mandatory to protect communication between the client and the server, ensuring that tokens and sensitive data are not intercepted. Configuring TLS certificates correctly, applying security policies at the server level and using HTTP headers that prevent XSS attacks and code injection are complementary measures that strengthen the infrastructure. In production environments, the application must be isolated in a secure network, with firewalls and access policies that limit exposure to external attacks.

When packaging the application for production, it is important that the environment is identical to the development environment to avoid conflicts. Docker containers offer this consistency, and using tools like Kubernetes allows you to manage clusters of containers in an automated way. Configuring persistent volumes, secrets, and network settings in Kubernetes ensures that the application is always ready to scale with demand. Orchestration with Kubernetes also makes it possible to implement automatic restart policies in case of failures, data backup and balanced load distribution, maintaining availability even in partial failure scenarios.

Another deployment strategy involves the use of serverless platforms or managed services that abstract the infrastructure, such as AWS Lambda (with API Gateway) or Google Cloud Run. These solutions are ideal for applications that do not require dedicated servers and benefit from automatic scaling without manual configuration. Although migrating to serverless environments requires adjustments to the way the application is packaged and dependencies, they offer a significant advantage in terms of cost and maintenance, especially for APIs with variable traffic.

The implementation of automated tests and continuous integration is essential to ensure that the deployment occurs without surprises. Pipelines that perform unit, integration and performance tests before deploying help identify regressions and failures. The use of containers in test environments that simulate the production environment allows you to validate that all configurations, environment variables and connections are correct. Furthermore, rollback strategies must be in place so that, if something goes wrong, the previous version of the application can be restored quickly, minimizing downtime and service interruption.

By combining all these practices, the FastAPI application is prepared to operate in high-demand environments, guaranteeing scalability and performance. Using ASGI servers such as uvicorn and hypercorn allows the application to benefit from the asynchronous pattern, while packaging with Docker and orchestration with Kubernetes ensures that the application is distributed efficiently across multiple nodes. Constant monitoring with metrics and log tools, combined with the implementation of security policies and the integration of automated tests, creates a resilient ecosystem that quickly responds to incidents and adapts to access spikes without compromising the user experience.

The journey to deployment and scalability involves creating an infrastructure that allows the organic growth of the application. Each layer, from initial configuration and packaging to monitoring and dynamic tuning, must be handled with rigor and attention to detail. Preparing for production requires eliminating any debug code, setting safe environment variables, and adopting logging policies that do not expose sensitive information. The use of ASGI servers optimizes the management of simultaneous connections, while the deployment strategy with Docker and Kubernetes allows the application to scale horizontally in an automated and resilient manner.

For teams operating in microservices environments, dividing responsibilities across different containers and using load balancers ensures that each service can scale independently, meeting demand without creating bottlenecks. This modular approach also facilitates maintenance, as updates to one service do not affect the others, and the deployment of new versions becomes a continuous process without significant interruptions.

Integration with monitoring services such as Prometheus and Grafana makes it possible to view application performance in real time and adjust resources as needed. Collecting detailed metrics such as response time, CPU usage, memory consumption, and error rate allows the team to quickly identify where bottlenecks are and implement improvements. This visibility not only increases application reliability, but also provides valuable data for decision-making about future infrastructure expansions or optimizations.

In summary, preparing a FastAPI application for production

and ensuring its scalability involves a series of integrated practices that range from initial configuration, choosing ASGI servers, packaging with Docker and orchestration with Kubernetes, to implementing monitoring and security strategies. Each step of the process must be carefully planned and executed so that the application can handle high volumes of access, respond quickly to incidents and maintain data integrity, all without compromising the end user experience.

By adopting a robust and scalable approach, development teams not only improve application performance and security, but also create a solid foundation for future evolutions and integrations. The architecture built with FastAPI, combined with modern deployment and scalability practices, becomes an ideal solution to face the challenges of the constantly evolving digital environment, ensuring that the application remains resilient, secure and responsive even in high demand scenarios.

CHAPTER 19. TESTING AND CODE QUALITY FOR WEB APIS

Developing robust web applications requires practices that go beyond coding and feature delivery. Automated tests and care for code quality form the basis for ensuring that each route, business rule and data flow behaves correctly, avoiding regressions and maintenance issues. In environments that use Python and FastAPI, the adoption of libraries such as pytest makes the process of creating and executing tests simpler and more effective, while code quality tools help identify inconsistencies, duplications and possible vulnerabilities.

The importance of automated testing becomes clear when considering the speed of delivery and the complexity of systems that constantly evolve. With each new feature, dependency update or refactoring, the risks of breaking existing functionality increase. Automated testing reduces this risk by enabling rapid validation at all levels: unit testing, integration testing and acceptance testing. In a team that practices continuous integration, with each commit, the test suite is run through a pipeline, ensuring that any issues are detected and fixed immediately. Furthermore, documentation of the expected behavior of routes and business rules can be inferred from the tests themselves.

Setting up test environments (pytest, etc.) in Python usually starts with installing pytest:

bash

```
pip install pytest
```

This library automatically searches for files and functions that follow conventions such as test_arquivo.py and test_minha_funcao. For projects using FastAPI, it is common to combine pytest with other extensions, such as pytest-asyncio, to handle asynchronous routes and dependencies. A good practice is to create a directory structure that organizes code and tests clearly:

plaintext

```
my_fastapi_project/
├── app/
│   ├── main.py
│   ├── routers/
│   ├── models/
│   │   └── ...
├── tests/
│   ├── test_items.py
│   ├── test_users.py
│   │   └── ...
└── requirements.txt
```

This separation helps keep the structure organized, allowing each part of the application to have its dedicated tests. In environments that require specific test data and configurations, including fixtures in pytest, defined in conftest.py or specific files, can provide temporary database instances, session objects, and HTTP clients. An example fixture to create an HTTP client:

python

```
# EXAMPLE 1
# STEP 1: Test conftest.py
import pytest
from fastapi.testclient import TestClient
```

```
from app.main import app

@pytest.fixture
def client():
    return TestClient(app)
```

TestClient simulates HTTP requests for routes defined in the application, allowing end-to-end testing without needing a real server. Thus, it is possible to check routes, input parameters, responses and even status codes. In a test_items.py test file, functions might look like:

python

```python
# EXAMPLE 2
# STEP 2: test items
def test_create_item(client):
    data = {"name": "Laptop", "price": 1299.0}
    response = client.post("/items", json=data)
    assert response.status_code == 201
    result = response.json()
    assert "id" in result
    assert result["name"] == "Laptop"

def test_get_item(client):
    # Creating an item first
    create_resp = client.post("/items", json={"name": "Pen",
"price": 1.2})
    item_id = create_resp.json()["id"]
    # Retrieving the item
    get_resp = client.get(f"/items/{item_id}")
    assert get_resp.status_code == 200
    fetched_item = get_resp.json()
    assert fetched_item["price"] == 1.2
```

These functions exemplify integration tests, validating both the creation and retrieval of items. If the application is asynchronous, it is possible to use pytest-asyncio and perform async tests with the appropriate syntax and configuration.

Good code coverage practices imply creating enough tests to ensure that every logical branch, route, and class is checked. Tools like coverage.py allow you to quantitatively measure how many lines or branches of code were executed by tests. It is common to integrate coverage.py to generate detailed reports, like this:

bash

```
pip install coverage
coverage run -m pytest
coverage report
coverage html
```

After execution, coverage generates reports that indicate the percentage of coverage and highlight untested lines, which helps the team locate points that need additional testing. However, the search for 100% coverage should not be the only criterion, as the quality of tests is more important than mere quantity. Still, maintaining a high level of coverage reduces the risk of unchecked patches where bugs can hide.

Tools for analysis and continuous integration, such as GitHub Actions, GitLab CI or Jenkins, allow the test pipeline to be automatically executed with each code push. The configuration includes stages that install dependencies, run tests and generate coverage reports. If any test fails or coverage falls below an established minimum level, the pipeline signals an error, preventing code merging. This causes the team to review and correct any problems before they affect the main basis of the project. A CI pipeline in GitLab could contain something similar to:

yaml

```
# EXAMPLE 3
# STEP 3: .gitlab-ci.yml

stages:
 - test

test-job:
  stage: test
  image: python:3.10
  script:
    - pip install -r requirements.txt
    - coverage run -m pytest
    - coverage report --fail-under=80
  artifacts:
   reports:
    junit: report.xml
   paths:
    - htmlcov/
```

In this file, the pipeline defines a stage test, which runs coverage and fails if coverage drops below 80%. Artifacts records XML reports (used in integrations with other tools) and generates the htmlcov directory containing the browsable report. This way, any team member can check what happened in the pipeline, analyzing logs and reports without having to run it locally.

Maintaining code quality involves not only testing, but also linters and formatters that standardize formatting, detect unused imports, and point out possible bad practices. Tools such as flake8, black, isort and mypy can be integrated into the pipeline, ensuring style and consistency are preserved. flake8 flags syntax and style issues, black automatically formats, isort organizes imports, and mypy checks static typing in Python. A flow of PRs, where changes go through code verification and testing, reinforces reliability before the feature goes into production.

Another point is the adoption of security and performance tests. Tools like locust and k6 can simulate load scenarios, sending thousands of requests per second to assess API resilience. When detecting throughput limits, the team optimizes the code or configures scalability strategies. Security tests, such as bandit, analyze the repository for common Python vulnerabilities, including use of insecure functions, mishandling of sensitive data, or improper access to external APIs.

Many complex systems, made up of microservices, require integration tests that validate how different services communicate. In such scenarios, it is useful to upload dependent services in Docker containers into CI pipelines, using docker-compose to orchestrate databases, message queues, and the application under test itself. This flow ensures that interactions are carried out with the same stack as in the real environment. If any bank migration or change in routes breaks the contract, the pipeline will fail, indicating regression.

Another type of verification that enriches project quality is based on contract testing, when there are front-ends or API consumers that require a stable interface. Contracts can be formalized in OpenAPI documents and verified with pact testing or other tools, ensuring that the API returns the expected fields and formats. If an endpoint removes a crucial field, contract tests detect it, preventing the introduction of silent breaks.

When running tests, it is recommended to isolate resources that may cause side effects, such as production databases, external APIs, and storage systems. Setting up mocks or stubs to replace external dependencies prevents tests from being slow, brittle, and affecting real data. In Python, the unittest.mock library and pytest monkeypatch are frequent allies in this task. In routes that call other services, creating mocks prevents any external instability from interrupting the verification flow.

In web APIs, acceptance or end-to-end tests can include scenarios that reproduce the user's journey, performing login, creating records, updates and searches. Using FastAPI's TestClient or external tools like Postman (Newman CLI) and Cypress helps verify that the API works correctly in a close-to-real environment. These tests are valuable for detecting integration issues, permission errors, or confusing flow. A Python library, such as pytest-bdd, makes it possible to write scenarios in business language (Gherkin), creating tests that are closer to the stakeholders' vocabulary.

Test suite maintenance requires discipline. When routes change, tests need to reflect the updated behavior. If a test becomes obsolete, it is best to remove or correct it to avoid false negatives or positives. This care ensures that the test suite remains relevant and reliable throughout the project lifecycle. A development team that sees value in testing and code quality tends to identify problems early, reducing rework and improving overall stability.

Continuous integration also extends to code review processes, where colleagues examine what has been written before approving the merge. Tools like GitHub Actions and GitLab CI display test and code analysis results in the pull request interface itself. If coverage has decreased, the pipeline fails or flags an alert for the PR author to add additional tests. If the linter encounters serious problems, correction becomes mandatory. This automation ecosystem makes the development flow more agile and robust, as each change undergoes rigorous validation without relying exclusively on manual reviews.

Another good practice involves maintaining a smoke test suite, made up of quick tests that check critical functionalities.

These tests can be performed in a few seconds, confirming that the main routes are operational, that the bank is accessible and that authentication works. This set reduces the likelihood of broken deploys reaching the end user. In parallel, more complete tests can be run in a nightly pipeline or staging environments.

Regarding code style, adopting automatic formatters like black and organizing imports with isort ensures consistency. These tools can run locally or in the CI pipeline, failing if they detect divergences. In the end, the project gains visual standardization and eliminates subjective discussions about style. This process complements the use of linters (e.g. flake8, pylint) that point out unused imports, undefined variables, and potential logic bugs. mypy, in turn, highlights typing issues in Python, ensuring that type annotations remain coherent.

A static code analysis system can be integrated to detect even more problems. Tools like SonarQube or CodeClimate evaluate complexity metrics, duplication, potential vulnerabilities, and security practices. These platforms generate scores that help the team track code quality developments and decide refactoring priorities. Methodologies such as Clean Code and SOLID can be actively observed, and static analysis provides alerts when the cyclomatic complexity of a method grows or when there are excessively nested sections.

Combining automated testing, high code coverage and continuous analysis, the development of web APIs gains solidity and predictability. Errors are caught before they affect the end user, refactoring becomes safe and the team has the confidence to evolve features without fear of regressions. In 2025, the growing demand for fast and resilient deliveries makes these pillars even more fundamental, as scalable and distributed systems require reliability in each component. A quality culture is consolidated when everyone realizes that testing and good practices do not slow down development, but accelerate it, avoiding rework and increasing user satisfaction.

It is useful to mention that, in the scenario of developing APIs with FastAPI, the adoption of OpenAPI contract testing and validation also stands out. If the application generates a / openapi.json file, it is possible to verify that each endpoint, model and parameter corresponds to what the client or other service expects. Pact testing tools or custom test libraries can consume this file, ensuring that there are no discrepancies between what the route announces and what it actually accepts or returns.

Many complex applications use mocks for external services, databases and even queues in order to speed up test execution. However, it is essential to keep integration tests running in a pipeline or staging environment, where everything is tested together. This balance between unit tests (fast and focused on a function or class) and integration tests (slower and more comprehensive) generates coverage of several scenarios, reducing the likelihood of failures going unnoticed. In cases of systems with microservices, a contract and end-to-end test suite ensures that the interaction between services does not suffer silent breakdowns.

A positive reflection of attention to code quality is the ease of onboarding new team members. A well-tested repository that follows formatting and style standards reduces the learning curve, as the code base remains clean and self-explanatory. Those who start contributing quickly understand the structure, know how to run the tests and what is expected in terms of PRs. On the other hand, projects without testing and standardization suffer from rework, recurring bugs and difficulties in evolution.

Another best practice for maintaining quality involves adopting feature branches and pull requests, where each significant change goes through the CI pipeline, runs tests, and can receive peer reviews. This flow prevents code smells and logic problems from accumulating in the main base, making refactoring much easier and more predictable. Implementing tagging in the repository, such as "needs tests" or "refactor required," helps control technical debt, addressing points that need future attention.

An often forgotten but relevant aspect is the creation of tests for error and validation scenarios. When building APIs with FastAPI, using Pydantic automatically validates fields and types, but it is essential to test how the application reacts to input that is incomplete, invalid, or exceeds limits. Checking that the route returns status code 422 with the appropriate message body ensures that API consumers receive correct feedback. It is also important to test custom exceptions and unauthorized access or non-existent route scenarios, ensuring that the application handles failures consistently.

Investing time in writing tests for each layer of the system, from the route to the data model, through business rules, is the key to a sustainable development pipeline. When the team includes tests in the daily flow, the probability of regressions drops drastically, and with each change the application becomes more stable. Continuous integration and coverage analysis reinforce this cycle, indicating what needs more attention. This virtuous cycle culminates in greater delivery speed, as fewer bugs are fixed after deployment, fewer hotfixes are released and the team is not drowning in emergency problems.

In cases where the application demands scalability, performance must also be tested with routes that simulate intensive use, querying databases, interacting with cache and orchestrating various dependencies. Stress and endurance tests detect memory leaks or points of contention that do not appear in common testing routines. Tools like locust and k6 can integrate with the pipeline, running load scenarios and generating latency and throughput reports. From this data, the team makes decisions about refactoring queries, expanding hardware or implementing caching.

Care for code quality and automated testing practices is reflected in systems that survive major evolutions, being able to incorporate new functionalities, correct problems and maintain a high degree of reliability even after years of development. Implementing code review and gating merge policies (where the pipeline prevents the merging of PRs that do not meet the testing and coverage criteria) prevents the repository from collapsing due to complexity and bugs.

In short, ensuring testing and code quality is an essential factor for APIs built with FastAPI or any other framework. Adopting test environments configured with pytest, striving for meaningful code coverage, and integrating with analytics and CI tools creates a virtuous cycle of development. Each commit goes through rigorous validations, and the application evolves safely. The result is cohesive, resilient and transparent code, where each route has its behavior specified and verified, each exception is handled, each business rule is confirmed, and consumers can trust the stability of the service. This panorama aligns with the requirements of 2025 and beyond, in which agility and reliability become crucial differentiators to compete and innovate in a constantly evolving market.

CHAPTER 20. GOOD PRACTICES AND CODE STANDARDS

Writing code in a consistent and standardized way not only makes it easier to maintain, it also improves readability and reduces the risk of errors. Adopting established standards such as PEP 8, practicing continuous refactoring and using static analysis tools are essential to ensure that code is understandable, scalable and efficient. Furthermore, the implementation of continuous integration and deployment (CI/CD) allows the development team to automate processes and maintain a robust workflow, minimizing failures.

A **adoption of standards** It's one of the first steps to establishing clean, organized code. PEP 8 is the official convention for writing Python code, covering everything from indentation rules to best practices for variable naming and import organization. One of the most basic guidelines in PEP 8 is the use of 4-space indentation, ensuring uniformity across the codebase:

python

```
# EXAMPLE 1
# STEP 1: PEP Code 8
def calculate_total(unit_price, quantity):
    total = unit_price * quantity
    return total
```

In addition to indentation, PEP 8 defines that variables and functions must be named in **snake_case**, while classes use **CamelCase**. Avoiding generic names or unnecessary abbreviations improves code readability:

python

```
# EXAMPLE 2
# STEP 2: Naming variables and functions
class Customer:
    def __init__(self, name, age):
        self.name = name
        self.age = age
```

Organizing imports correctly is also an essential aspect. PEP 8 recommends separating them into three groups:

1. **Standard library imports**
2. **Imports from third-party libraries**
3. **Internal project imports**

The correct order avoids confusion and makes reading easier:

python

```
# EXAMPLE 3
# STEP 3: Organization of imports
import them
import sys

import requests

from app.models import Usuario
```

As **refactoring and maintenance techniques** are critical to keeping the code efficient as the application grows. The principle **DRY (Don't Repeat Yourself)** suggests that duplicate code should be eliminated whenever possible, replacing redundant blocks with reusable functions.

A code that repeats logic unnecessarily:

python

```
# EXAMPLE 4
# STEP 4: Repetitive (bad) code
total_price = unit_price * quantity
print(f"Total: {preco_total}")

total_discount = discount * quantity
print(f"Discount: {discount_total}")
```

Can be refactored to:

python

```
# EXAMPLE 5
# STEP 5: Optimized code with function
def calculate_value(price, quantity):
    return price * quantity

print(f"Total: {calcular_value(unit_price, quantity)}")
print(f"Discount: {calcular_value(discount, quantity)}")
```

Function decomposition and modularization also contribute to readability and scalability. Keeping functions small and focused on a single responsibility improves testability and reduces complexity.

A **continuous integration and deployment (CI/CD)** are essential for automating the development lifecycle. Tools such as GitHub Actions, GitLab CI/CD and Jenkins ensure that tests are automatically executed with each change to the code, preventing the introduction of bugs before deployment. A basic CI/CD pipeline might include the following steps:

1. **Installation of dependencies**
2. **Executing automated tests**
3. **Code coverage check**
4. **Automatic deployment if all tests pass**

An example CI/CD pipeline using GitHub Actions:

yaml

```yaml
# EXAMPLE 6
# STEP 6: Pipeline file in GitHub Actions
name: CI/CD Pipeline

on:
  push:
    branches:
      - main

jobs:
  build:
    runs-on: ubuntu-latest

    steps:
      - name: Repository checkout
        uses: actions/checkout@v3

      - name: Environment configuration
        run: pip install -r requirements.txt

      - name: Test execution
        run: pytest

      - name: Automatic deployment
        if: success()
        run: ./deploy.sh
```

This pipeline checks whether the tests pass before deploying. If an error is detected, the action fails and the code is not sent to production.

A **use of static analysis tools** automates code quality checking, ensuring standards are followed and reducing the risk of hidden problems. Tools like **flake8, black e mypy** can be integrated into the CI/CD pipeline to ensure code is well formatted and free from typos.

THE **flake8** detects problems such as incorrect indentation, unused variables and bad practices:

bash

```
pip install flake8
flake8 my_project/
```

THE **black** automatically formats the code, ensuring standardization:

bash

```
pip install black
black my_project/
```

THE **mypy** analyzes static typing, detecting possible errors even before execution:

bash

```
pip install mypy
mypy my_project/
```

By integrating these tools with CI/CD, any issues in the code are identified before they are merged into the main branch.

Maintaining clean and organized code is not just a matter of aesthetics, but a determining factor for the scalability and maintenance of the application. Adopting standards like PEP 8, constantly refactoring to avoid redundancies, and integrating quality tools into the workflow are essential steps to ensuring that code remains understandable, efficient, and secure over time. Using CI/CD, static analysis, and automated formatting not only speeds up development, but also reduces the likelihood of errors reaching the production environment, making the development process more predictable and reliable.

CHAPTER 21. DEBUGGING AND MONITORING IN WEB APPLICATIONS

Developing robust web applications faces challenges in identifying and fixing bugs, as well as maintaining optimal performance and preventing unexpected outages. Even experienced teams encounter situations where the application works perfectly in one environment, but encounters subtle problems in production. The adoption of effective debugging practices, combined with constant monitoring, is essential to preserve the health of the system. Advanced debugging techniques allow you to identify bottlenecks, silent and intermittent failures, while logs and Application Performance Monitoring (APM) tools help with performance analysis and incident tracking.

The adoption of **advanced debugging techniques** It ranges from careful log analysis to the use of profiling tools that identify functions or code snippets that consume resources unnecessarily. In Python, it is common to use breakpoints to inspect the state of the application at key moments, interrupting execution and checking variable values. Adding the breakpoint() command at strategic points in the code or using debuggers in the IDE (such as PyCharm and Visual Studio Code) help discover inconsistencies that don't arise in superficial logs.

A simple example of using a breakpoint in a route segment:

python

```python
# EXAMPLE 1
# STEP 1: route with breakpoint
from fastapi import FastAPI

app = FastAPI()

@app.get("/debug")
def debug_route():
    x = 10
    y = 20
    breakpoint()  # Execution will pause here in debugging mode
    return {"result": x + y}
```

When running the application in debug mode, the debugger stops execution at the breakpoint, allowing it to examine the environment. In production environments, the practice of inserting breakpoints or print statements should be used with caution, as they may reveal sensitive information or impair performance. Still, analysis locally or in a staging environment with detailed logs is often essential for reproducing and fixing complex errors.

Another valuable approach to debugging is **instrumentation** of code with custom counters and metrics. By spreading counters or annotations that record how many times a function is called, how long it takes and what parameters it receives, the team now has data to identify anomalous behaviors or bottlenecks. Many libraries **observability** facilitate this process, integrating the collected data into dashboards where the team can see spikes in access or functions that dominate CPU usage.

Remote debugging techniques, using libraries such as **debugpy** and orchestrated container environments also allow you to connect debuggers to instances running on the server, examining issues that only appear in production. This practice may require extra configuration to ensure security. An example route to enable remote debugging would integrate with the pipeline, but should generally be disabled in normal production:

python

```
# EXAMPLE 2
# STEP 2: excerpt for remote debugging
import debugpy

def enable_remote_debug():
    # Listen on 0.0.0.0:5678
    debugpy.listen(("0.0.0.0", 5678))
    print("Remote debug listening on port 5678, awaiting
attach...")
    debugpy.wait_for_client()
```

It is essential that access to this service is restricted to prevent attackers from gaining full control of the application. In this scenario, remote debugging tools can help capture the failure in a staging environment that faithfully simulates production.

Performance monitoring and logs is the second major pillar. Systematic log collection simplifies incident troubleshooting and trend analysis. In Python applications, logging libraries are configured by declaring log levels (DEBUG, INFO, WARNING, ERROR, CRITICAL), storing logs in files or sending them to services such as Elasticsearch. A minimalist log configuration snippet:

python

```
# EXAMPLE 3
# STEP 3: basic logging configuration
import logging
```

```
logging.basicConfig(
    level=logging.INFO,
    format='%(asctime)s [%(levelname)s] %(name)s: %
(message)s'
)

logger = logging.getLogger(__name__)

def process_data(data):
    logger.info(f"Processing data: {data}")
    # ...
```

Upon execution, each log generates a line that includes the level, logger name, and message. In complex environments, logs are directed to aggregation and analysis platforms such as **Graylog, Splunk ou Elastic Stack**, ensuring the team can filter and correlate events over time. If a spike in 500 errors appears on an endpoint, you can easily investigate the stack trace and see the history of requesters, guiding corrective actions.

Performance monitoring is enriched with **APM (Application Performance Monitoring) tools**, like **New Relic, Datadog, Sentry or Prometheus**. These solutions collect latency metrics, CPU and memory usage, request count, error rate and even transaction tracking. In FastAPI systems, instrumentation is straightforward, as several libraries support route interception. This makes it possible to observe the time spent on each layer (database, cache, external calls), identifying bottlenecks or endpoints that take longer than normal. An example of integration with Prometheus:

python

```
# EXAMPLE 4
# STEP 4: Integration with Prometheus
from prometheus_fastapi_instrumentator import
Instrumentator
```

```
from fastapi import FastAPI

app = FastAPI()

Instrumentator().instrument(app).expose(app, endpoint="/
metrics")
```

With this, a /metrics endpoint is created, exposing usage statistics that can be collected by a Prometheus server and later displayed in a Grafana dashboard. Metrics include average response time, number of requests per route, returned status codes, and other valuable information. In 2025, the adoption of this type of visibility will become almost mandatory for any system that needs to remain competitive and reliable.

Analysis Tools (APM, remote monitoring) also include solutions such as Sentry, which captures exceptions, generates alerts and provides a detailed failure history, displaying environment variables, stack trace and even the affected user. Integrating the application with Sentry is simple, just install the library and configure:

python

```
# EXAMPLE 5
# STEP 5: Basic integration with Sentry
import sentry_sdk
from fastapi import FastAPI
from sentry_sdk.integrations.asgi import
SentryAsgiMiddleware

sentry_sdk.init(dsn="https://chave_sentry@sentry.io/
projeto_id", traces_sample_rate=1.0)

app = FastAPI()
app.add_middleware(SentryAsgiMiddleware)
```

Any unhandled exception generates a record in Sentry, with extensive context detail, making it easier to identify the root cause and prioritize corrections. This reduces incident response time as developers receive alerts via email or chat channels in real time.

Incident response strategies they are equally crucial for dealing with inevitable failures. Even with comprehensive testing and good processes, problems arise in production. A well-defined response plan provides concrete steps: identify the problem, analyze logs or APM, activate responsible teams, escalate if necessary and keep stakeholders informed. In some cases, automation can detect spikes in latency or error rate and initiate rollback, traffic redirection or autoscaling processes, ensuring service continuity without waiting for manual intervention.

An incident management flow can follow the following structure:

1. **Detection:** Monitoring or logs detect an increase in errors or latency.
2. **Notification:** Alert tool (PagerDuty, OpsGenie, etc.) alerts the team on duty.
3. **Diagnosis:** Engineers use logs, APM, and remote debugging to find the root cause.
4. **Mitigation:** If possible, rolling back or scaling resources alleviates the impact immediately.
5. **Correction:** Configuration adjustments or code patches are implemented.
6. **Validation:** New tests and monitoring confirm the resolution of the problem.
7. **Retrospective:** The incident is documented and the process is improved to avoid recurrence.

The adoption of methodologies such as **post-mortems** helps extract valuable lessons from each incident, continually improving system robustness. Mature teams avoid pointing out blame and focus on systemic fixes, automations and improvements to the detection process.

In distributed applications based on microservices, debugging and monitoring become even more critical. Each service depends on several others, and problems can arise in interfaces, timeouts and message queues. Distributed tracing tools, such as **Jaeger** or **Zipkin**, allow you to track the journey of each request through different services, helping to locate where delays or failures occur. A transaction might start at the gateway, go through service A, trigger service B, and write something to service C. If one of them is responding slowly, tracing will show that leg as a bottleneck. Python configuration can use libraries like opentelemetry:

python

```python
# EXAMPLE 6
# STEP 6: Opentelemetry tracing
from opentelemetry import trace
from opentelemetry.sdk.resources import Resource
from opentelemetry.sdk.trace import TracerProvider
from opentelemetry.sdk.trace.export import
BatchSpanProcessor, ConsoleSpanExporter
from fastapi import FastAPI

resource = Resource(attributes={"service.name": "my-fastapi-service"})
provider = TracerProvider(resource=resource)
processor = BatchSpanProcessor(ConsoleSpanExporter())
provider.add_span_processor(processor)
trace.set_tracer_provider(provider)

app = FastAPI()

@app.get("/trace")
def trace_route():
```

```
tracer = trace.get_tracer(__name__)
with tracer.start_as_current_span("my-span"):
    return {"message": "Tracing example"}
```

This setup generates spans that can be sent to a remote tracing collector, such as Jaeger, allowing you to view the complete flow of requests. In advanced scenarios, each route and each call to external services receive spans, generating a visual map of how the request propagates. The team can then immediately identify which service needs optimization or if one is unavailable.

In this way, debugging and monitoring take on multiple layers: local logs, APM tools, distributed tracing, performance metrics and incident management processes. Each layer brings different information, and the sum of them builds a holistic view of the application. Adopting a pipeline for collecting and analyzing logs, metrics and tracing allows the team to quickly react to any abnormal behavior, minimizing impacts to the end user.

When talking about systems in 2025, the agility in development and the complexity of architectures require a proactive monitoring stance. It's not just about solving problems after they occur, but about predicting risk situations, implementing preventive alerts for spikes in usage or performance degradation. Machine Learning tools for log analysis can detect atypical patterns and alert before a critical incident occurs. Although this practice is still evolving, large companies are already using it to drastically reduce their mean time to resolution (MTTR).

Another important detail is the staging environments and feature flags for more controlled debugging. By activating a feature flag, the team releases certain functionality to a small group of users or even to itself, analyzing logs and performance data in real time. If something goes wrong, just disable the flag. This method avoids deploying untested functionality to the entire user base, drastically reducing large-scale incidents.

The interaction between development and operations teams, known as DevOps, reinforces the need for constant collaboration. Software engineers and SRE (Site Reliability Engineering) work together to ensure that each component can be observed, debugged and scaled. Sharing dashboards and daily reports allows everyone to stay informed about the health of the system. Log review ceremonies, post-mortems and capacity planning become a routine part, ensuring continuous collective learning.

Ultimately, debugging and monitoring in web applications are dynamic processes, as each version change, each increase in users or each service integration can introduce new behaviors. Adopting observability pipelines and a hands-on debugging mindset allows the team to anticipate potential problems, keep quality under control, and respond promptly to any failures. This proactive and carefully planned mentality, combined with advanced tools, allows applications to remain competitive and reliable in an increasingly demanding and accelerated market scenario.

In short, advanced debugging practices combine breakpoints, instrumentation, and detailed logging to uncover subtle flaws. Continuous performance monitoring, through logs, metrics and APM, alerts the team about degradation or anomalies, while distributed tracing solutions clarify how requests traverse microservices. Specialized tools like Sentry and Prometheus simplify error tracking and metrics collection. All of this is complemented with incident management strategies, ensuring not only that the team quickly identifies problems, but also that they can mitigate them and learn from them, continually refining the system's resilience.

CHAPTER 22. MICROSERVICES WITH FLASK AND FASTAPI

The microservices model has gained popularity for facilitating the maintenance and scalability of web systems, allowing each service to be developed, deployed and scaled independently. In 2025, the market is looking for more modular and resilient architectures, aimed at continuous and fast deliveries. Python frameworks, such as Flask and FastAPI, fit well in this context, as they allow you to build lightweight and efficient services, each responsible for a specific part of the application. Adopting a distributed architecture brings benefits in terms of flexibility and fault isolation, but it also introduces challenges in communication between components, monitoring and orchestration.

You **concepts and advantages of microservices** They start from the idea of dividing a monolithic application into several smaller services, each focused on a functional domain, such as authentication, payment processing, catalog management or sending notifications. Instead of a central code that concentrates all business rules, an ecosystem of independent services is created that communicate through simple protocols, usually HTTP/REST or messaging. Each microservice can be written in a different language, scaled individually according to demand or have a separate development life cycle, allowing teams to act in parallel without impacting other parts of the system.

Fault isolation is another advantage, because if a specific service has problems or is unavailable, the rest of the application can continue operating. This resilience, however, depends on error-tolerant communication layers, load balancers and practices such as circuit breakers. The microservices approach also allows the team to select the ideal technology for each part of the system, be it Flask or FastAPI for HTTP routes, machine learning libraries for intensive processing, or even different languages, as long as there are clear communication contracts.

A **distributed architecture and communication between services** demands consistent standards. Many teams adopt RESTful APIs over HTTP, exchanging data in JSON or Protobuf. In high-volume scenarios, messaging with brokers such as RabbitMQ, Kafka or NATS becomes relevant, as it frees services from always being online at the same time, operating asynchronously and increasing scalability. In Python, frameworks like Flask and FastAPI are excellent for building services that expose routes, while messaging libraries allow you to scale communications. The gateway or orchestrator that unifies routes and manages service discovery also gains importance. This gateway handles conditional routing, centralized authentication, and request limits.

A common solution is to use a **API Gateway**. In some architectures, this gateway filters external requests and redirects them to the correct microservice. The application of Flask or FastAPI in each microservice is responsible only for domain-specific routes. For example, a payments microservice offers /payments and /refund, a users microservice offers /users and /profile, and so on. The gateway is responsible for unifying subpaths and managing authentication, tokens and rate limiting. This design prevents each service from needing to reinvent its entire security logic.

Each microservice defines its **contract** communication, typically using OpenAPI (Swagger) or Protobuf. If the team standardizes on JSON with OpenAPI, documentation and testability maintenance is simplified. It is useful to maintain independent repositories for each service or monorepos containing all parts of the system with clear separations. Versions and deployment follow their own pipelines, allowing only one service to be updated without impacting the rest.

A **implementation of independent services** With Flask and FastAPI it is similar to creating a monolithic application, but with a much smaller scope. Each service focuses on a specific set of routes and business rules. The first step, for example, is to create a catalog microservice that manages products, and another for orders that receives order creation requests. Communication between them can occur via REST or queue, depending on consistency requirements. By 2025, the use of *event-driven architecture* has grown because it simplifies scalability by allowing each service to generate events that others can react to.

A microservice in FastAPI that manages products:

python

```python
# EXAMPLE 1
# STEP 1: Catalog microservice
from fastapi import FastAPI, HTTPException

app = FastAPI()

products_db = [
    {"id": 1, "name": "Laptop", "price": 1200.00, "stock": 10},
    {"id": 2, "name": "Mouse", "price": 25.50, "stock": 100},
]

@app.get("/products")
def list_products():
    return products_db

@app.get("/products/{product_id}")
def get_product(product_id: int):
    for product in products_db:
```

```
        if product["id"] == product_id:
            return product
    raise HTTPException(status_code=404, detail="Product
not found")

@app.post("/products")
def create_product(name: str, price: float, stock: int):
    new_id = len(products_db) + 1
    product = {"id": new_id, "name": name, "price": price,
"stock": stock}
    products_db.append(product)
    return product
```

This catalog service defines simple routes: listing, searching and creating products. It can run in isolation with uvicorn, responding on a defined port. Another microservice, for example, responsible for orders, would consume this catalog service to check availability or update stock. Communication can be via HTTP, calling the /products or /products/{id} endpoint and parsing JSON. If the team opts for messaging, the ordering microservice would publish an "OrderCreated" event to which the catalog service would react, decrementing inventory.

An ordering microservice:

python

```
# EXAMPLE 2
# STEP 2: Ordering microservice
from fastapi import FastAPI, HTTPException
import requests

app = FastAPI()

orders_db = []

@app.post("/orders")
```

```
def create_order(product_id: int, quantity: int):
    product_service_url = "http://catalog:8000/products" #
supposed catalog microservice DNS
    product_resp = requests.get(f"{product_service_url}/
{product_id}")
    if product_resp.status_code != 200:
        raise HTTPException(status_code=404, detail="Product
not found")

    product_data = product_resp.json()
    if product_data["stock"] < quantity:
        raise HTTPException(status_code=400,
detail="Insufficient stock")

    # Logic for creating order
    new_id = len(orders_db) + 1
    order = {
        "id": new_id,
        "product_id": product_data["id"],
        "quantity": quantity,
        "total": product_data["price"] * quantity
    }
    orders_db.append(order)

    # Update inventory in catalog microservice
    # In a robust design, this update could be done via POST or
PUT
    # or by publishing an "OrderCreated" event
    # Here it is exemplified by calling associated route
    product_data["stock"] -= quantity
    # this update route is not in the previous example, but it
could exist
    return order
```

This implementation shows two services interacting via HTTP requests. The ordering microservice calls the catalog route to check the product. In container environments, internal DNS or service discovery defines the URL (e.g., "http://catalog:8000"). This style of integration is simple, but latency and potential network failures need to be addressed. In highly complex scenarios, the adoption of queues or patterns such as saga and circuit breaker becomes essential.

Each microservice runs its own **database**, as microservices do not usually share structures in a coupled way. This independence is crucial to enable scalability and maintain clear boundaries of responsibility. The orchestration of containers for these services, including load balancers, logs, monitoring, is done with Docker Compose or Kubernetes, defining each service in its deployment and using internal routes or ingress controllers to expose endpoints.

You **practical cases and common challenges** of microservices appear in data synchronization, integration testing and observability. If the ordering service updates the inventory in the catalog and the catalog fails midway through the ordering process, the system may be in an inconsistent state. In this scenario, rollback patterns or transactional messaging help, requiring careful design. Testing an isolated microservice locally is simple, but ensuring the entire suite works requires end-to-end or contractual test scenarios, where each service defines its OpenAPI and interactions are simulated. In 2025, the automation of this flow is essential to avoid regressions.

To handle logs across multiple services, it is common to centralize them in a stack like **ELK (Elasticsearch, Logstash, Kibana)** or another solution that aggregates and facilitates searches. Measuring performance and error rates in microservices is integrated with APM systems, generating graphs and alerts for each component. The adoption of distributed tracing with **Jaeger or Zipkin** makes it easier to discover slow routes in call chains. Each microservice must expose metrics and logs that reflect health, CPU usage, memory and request latency, all easily consolidated into a dashboard.

In terms of security, each microservice requires appropriate authentication and authorization configurations. You can implement a central authentication service (Auth Service) that issues JWT tokens, and each microservice validates this token in requests. In Flask and FastAPI applications, it is simple to create dependencies or middleware that check user tokens and roles. This design avoids duplication of logic and creates consistency in access control. A common pitfall is not clearly defining the boundaries of what each microservice should take care of, resulting in couplings or duplications, something that contradicts the microservice philosophy.

Another issue is the standardization of messaging style. If the team uses JSON, consistent conventions must be adopted for naming fields, encodings and status codes, ensuring that clients and other services understand the data. If gRPC is adopted, the Protobufs definition maintains strong typing and removes ambiguity. However, this style requires an HTTP proxy or specialized SDKs, which can be more complex depending on the team.

To orchestrate releases and avoid interruptions, adopting **blue-green deployments** or **canary releases** ensures that new releases are tested with part of the traffic before reaching all users. In a microservices ecosystem, each service can be updated separately, as long as it maintains backwards compatibility. CI/CD and container registry tools integrate this flow, creating Docker images and testing them in pipelines.

Horizontal scalability of each service becomes simple when isolating each one in containers. One of the biggest differences of microservices is the ability to allocate more replicas only to the part of the system that is under pressure. If the payments microservice receives more requests, it can be scaled from 3 to 10 replicas, while the catalog service remains at

2 replicas. The orchestrator (Kubernetes, ECS, etc.) manages traffic distribution, and autoscaling is driven by CPU, latency, or throughput metrics. This dynamic sizing avoids wasted resources, generating savings and being resilient to seasonal peaks.

However, the **microservices complexity** is not negligible. In addition to multiple repositories and the individual CI/CD pipeline, the team has to maintain deployment scripts for each component, manage logs and distributed tracking. The learning curve can be steep, especially if the team is migrating from a monolith to microservices. Inconsistencies in data modeling, REST contracts, and event handling can result in failures that are difficult to track. Therefore, the adoption of microservices is only justified in projects where the independence and differentiated scheduling of parts of the system bring significant gains in relation to the maintenance of a well-organized monolith.

One **practical case** common: an e-commerce company that handles product catalogue, shopping cart, payment processing and sending emails. Each service implemented with Flask or FastAPI manages its development cycle and can be versioned separately. The catalog team can expand the way they display product attributes without affecting the cart team, and this team can restructure the checkout flow without impacting the payment gateway, as long as they respect the endpoint agreement. With this design, the company benefits from team autonomy, only scheduling the checkout service during periods of high traffic (for example, Black Friday), keeping costs under control.

Along the way, challenges arise. If the catalog service and the cart service differ in JSON format or routes, the entire application becomes fragile. Adopt **well-defined contracts** and integration testing forms the basis of a robust pipeline. When the cart team changes something, it runs tests against the catalog service mock and vice versa, preventing silent breaks from reaching production. Orchestration, done via Docker Compose in development environments and Kubernetes in production, simplifies local reproduction of the ecosystem.

A **resilience** It's another topic: when one service depends on another, if the called service becomes unavailable, the application must handle the situation gracefully. Patterns such as circuit breaker and fallback responses become necessary. The circuit breaker monitors failures and, if it detects repeated unsuccessful attempts, it aborts calls for a while, avoiding overloading the failed service and freeing up resources for other routes. Fallback can provide cached or degraded data without breaking the entire user experience.

A **observability** ensures the identification of problems in microservices. Each service records logs and metrics locally, but an aggregation system like ELK Stack (Elasticsearch, Logstash and Kibana) or Splunk unifies this information, enabling searches and correlations. Tracing distributed via Jaeger or Zipkin tracks requests that transit through different services. So, if an order fails at the payment stage, it is simple to see that the /checkout route called /payments and then / inventory, and notice if there was a 500 error in /inventory, for example. Without this tracing, debugging would be much more complex.

A **authentication** Centralized technology also stands out: instead of each service running its own login logic and tokens, an Identity Provider (IdP) or an authentication and authorization microservice is defined that issues JWT tokens. The other services validate tokens and extract roles or permissions from the payload. This design avoids duplicating security logic. At the same time, care must be taken with latency and token expiration. It is common to use gateways and caches for tokens on a large scale.

Us **common challenges**, there is network overhead, the

difficulty of integrated testing, the need for orchestration and the complexity of distributed logs. It is essential to plan the network topology: each microservice must know URLs or discovery service addresses, if adopted. Local tests must simulate the ecosystem, creating containers for each service and its dependencies. Logs and traces need to be configured so that the team does not get lost when investigating problems. Without these precautions, the adoption of microservices can become a debugging and orchestration nightmare.

In 2025, the trend of composing microservices with minimalist frameworks like Flask and FastAPI remains strong, as their lightness and simplicity fit well with the proposal of each service being small and focused. The adoption of FastAPI, in particular, brings advantages in terms of automatic typing and documentation, simplifying route construction and communication with other services. Using Pydantic to validate data between services ensures that compatibility issues are identified quickly.

Another growing topic is the adoption of **serverless**. Instead of keeping processes running continuously, teams create functions triggered by events or HTTP requests, scaling from zero to hundreds of instances in seconds. Flask and FastAPI can be adapted to serverless platforms, but this requires modifying the way they are packaged and how they handle routes and state. In serverless microservices, each function is an isolated component, and the orchestration is up to the cloud. This style reduces the overhead of managing servers, but can add latency on cold starts and create state management challenges.

Finally, the **observance of good practices** and monitoring project evolution ensures that the distributed architecture remains sustainable. Microservices should not be a justification for excessively fragmenting the system into dozens of trivial services. The ideal size of each microservice depends on the domain and team, and the adoption of semantic boundaries (bounded contexts) is highly recommended. By keeping each service well defined and without overlapping responsibilities, the application maintains cohesion and minimizes interdependence.

In conclusion, adopting microservices with Flask and FastAPI is a promising strategy for building modular, scalable, and resilient systems. Each service focuses on a specific domain and can be developed and deployed at different paces. Communication can occur via HTTP or messaging, requiring standardization of formats and careful handling of failures. Well-executed design delivers scalability and agility, but requires orchestration and monitoring, as well as an automation and DevOps mindset. In the end, teams that embrace microservices and apply best practices in logging, distributed tracing, CI/CD and API governance reap the benefits of a system that evolves without becoming a cumbersome monolith, quickly adapting to changing market demands.

CHAPTER 23. MODERN WEB APPLICATION ARCHITECTURES

The development of advanced web applications involves choosing architectures that support rapid evolution, scalability and integration with diverse services. In 2025, the heterogeneity of platforms, languages and infrastructures demands increasingly flexible and modular solutions. Patterns like MVC and MVVM remain relevant, but modern practices also encompass microservices, containers, cloud orchestration, and complex integrations. Adopting an adequate architectural design impacts the system's ability to adapt to market demands, as well as maintain quality, security and performance over time.

You **architectural patterns (MVC, MVVM, etc.)** They emerged as a way to organize the code so that each responsibility is clear. MVC (Model-View-Controller) has historically been popular in frameworks like Rails and Django. It separates data (Model), presentation (View) and control logic (Controller). On the other hand, MVVM (Model-View-ViewModel) stands out in front-end scenarios, especially when JavaScript frameworks such as Vue.js or React (with Redux) adopt the idea of separating the data layer from the view layer through a ViewModel that manages state.

For large Python applications, traditional MVC can be distributed into distinct modules. The Model relates to database classes or entities, the Controller defines routes and business logic and the View can be replaced by templates (in the case of server-side frameworks) or by an API that serves data to front-end clients. In modern architectures, this separation is not always so strict. For example, in microservices, each service encapsulates its own Model and Controller logic, without necessarily having server-side Views, as the display usually occurs in decoupled front-ends.

In applications that combine dynamic front-end and lightweight back-end, MVVM is applied more at the front, with a JavaScript framework managing local state. The backend, in turn, only exposes API routes to manipulate data. This design takes advantage of JavaScript's ability to provide rich, responsive interfaces, while the server remains focused on serving JSON and managing data persistence. In critical systems, the choice between MVC and MVVM depends on factors such as volume of requests, real-time needs and team size. No standard is universally superior; each brings advantages in specific scenarios.

A **service integration and scalability** becomes crucial as the system grows and connects to external APIs, payment solutions, messaging tools, and other backend layers. Many modern web applications are, in practice, integration hubs, orchestrating data between different sources. Horizontal scalability, through replicas of the server that serves HTTP requests, ensures that traffic spikes are absorbed without overloading a single instance. Frameworks like Flask and FastAPI respond well in scaled environments, as they can run multiple workers managed by WSGI or ASGI servers.

However, scalability is not limited to the HTTP layer. Many systems adopt queues (RabbitMQ, Kafka) to process asynchronous tasks, reducing apparent latency for the user and distributing the workload among multiple workers. This design composes an event-driven architecture, facilitating the creation of data pipelines and the distribution of processing. The front end or an asynchronous API service sends messages to the queue, and other services, written in Python or any other language, consume these events and perform tasks such as generating reports, sending emails, or stock updates.

THE use of containers and orchestration (Docker, Kubernetes) It has radically changed the way web applications are deployed and managed. Docker provides standardized packaging for each service, containing its operating system, libraries and dependencies. This container can run on any supported host, ensuring repeatability and reducing environment conflicts. A typical Dockerfile for a Python application might be written like this:

dockerfile

```
# EXAMPLE 1
FROM python:3.10-slim

WORKDIR /app
COPY requirements.txt /app/
RUN pip install --no-cache-dir -r requirements.txt

COPY . /app

CMD ["python", "main.py"]
```

This container encapsulates the application, allowing it to run locally, on physical servers or in the cloud. When the application becomes composed of multiple containers (database, cache, authentication services), Docker Compose or Kubernetes takes over the orchestration, defining how each container connects and scales. In Docker Compose, a YAML file describes each service, its ports, and volumes:

yaml

```
# EXAMPLE 2
version: "3"
services:
  web:
```

```
build: .
ports:
  - "8000:8000"
depends_on:
  - db
db:
  image: postgres:14
  environment:
    POSTGRES_USER: user
    POSTGRES_PASSWORD: pass
```

In Kubernetes, resources are defined through objects such as Deployments and Services, which manage replicas and traffic routing. The Kubernetes cluster can run on cloud providers, ensuring automatic scaling based on CPU or latency metrics. In a Deploy, we specify the Docker image and how many replicas we want, while a Service defines how other parts of the cluster communicate with this set of pods.

Orchestration with Kubernetes, ECS (AWS), or another container provider in 2025 has become the de facto standard as it facilitates continuous updates, rollback, autoscaling, and integrated monitoring. Combined with CI/CD pipelines, the team can release new versions transparently, redirecting traffic only after confirming that everything works, or merging gradually to check for errors.

A **comparison between different approaches** can be summarized in the categories: monolith vs microservices, MVC vs MVVM frameworks, and containers vs traditional virtual machines. In a monolith, the application concentrates all functionalities in a single code and repository, simplifying initial development and deployment, but making scalability and team autonomy difficult as the project grows. In microservices, each part of the system is isolated, gaining scalability and independence, but at the cost of greater orchestration complexity and distributed communications.

As for frameworks and patterns, MVC is more traditional in back-ends that render server-side pages, while MVVM (or MV*) fits into complex front-ends, separating states and data from the view and allowing reactivity. However, hybrid teams simply adopt RESTful, GraphQL, or websockets to deliver data, while the presentation logic lives on the front-end with React or Vue. What defines the adoption of one pattern or another are the team's preferences, project history and interactivity and performance requirements.

When comparing containers and virtual machines, containers are lighter, start quickly and allow homogeneous packaging of dependencies, but they do not offer the same level of isolation as VMs, although, in practice, this isolation is sufficient for most scenarios. VMs, on the other hand, are independent at the operating system level, but have higher overhead in terms of resources and boot time. By 2025, most cloud services and DevOps pipelines will revolve around containers and orchestration as they simplify developer life and enable elastic scaling.

In highly complex scenarios, variations arise. Serverless architectures, offered by platforms like AWS Lambda or Google Cloud Functions, abstract the server layer completely, scaling to zero and running only when events occur. Comparing serverless to containers, serverless eliminates orchestration management and reduces costs for event-driven loads, but the latency of cold starts and runtime limitations can be impediments for services that demand constant response.

Another aspect to consider is the adoption of**Service Mesh**, like Istio or Linkerd, when working with microservices running on Kubernetes. Service Mesh introduces sidecar proxies into each pod, managing mutual authentication, intelligent routing, and telemetry transparently. The advantage is that security and observability functions are unified in the mesh, without polluting the application code.

The downside is the additional complexity, as managing and configuring Istio requires knowing CRDs (Custom Resource Definitions) and advanced configurations.

Some teams choose to **event-based architectures** or **CQRS (Command Query Responsibility Segregation)** for complex domains. The first case decentralizes the flow, each service reacts to events that arise in a broker like Kafka, which facilitates integration and extensibility. The disadvantage is eventual consistency and the possibility of lost messages if the broker is not configured correctly. CQRS separates reads and writes into distinct models, allowing high performance in queries, but requiring synchronization pipelines. In Python systems, frameworks that support this design are less common, so the implementation is customized, based on persistence and event orchestration libraries.

Architectures that combine containers, microservices and MVC/MVVM are quite flexible. For example, a team that creates a React front-end (MV*) consumes APIs from a microservice developed with FastAPI that follows a pattern of routes without rendering templates. Another microservice, focused on reporting, can use Flask to expose CSV routes, while a third handles asynchronous tasks in Celery. They all run in containers, orchestrated by Docker Compose locally and Kubernetes in production. Each container defines its CI/CD scaling and pipeline.

When it comes to scalability, the adoption of caching and database shards or NoSQL may be necessary as the system grows. In 2025, the polyglot approach to data is common: one microservice uses Postgres for transactions and another stores logs in Elasticsearch or objects in S3. The gateway or front-end aggregates everything, and the application displays complex insights. The orchestration ensures that each component is healthy, and if one crashes, the gateway routes that depend on it can fall back or say the service is unavailable, without taking the rest down.

It is important to note that, despite the diversity of modern architectures, planning and documenting each decision is essential to avoid chaos. Domain-Driven Design (DDD) practices and the definition of bounded contexts help to delimit the responsibility of each microservice or module. The adoption of distributed logging, tracing, and centralized telemetry ensures that if something goes wrong, the team quickly locates the source of the problem. The team must orchestrate deployments and versioning of APIs, ensuring compatibility or use of blue-green / canary releases to allow safe rollback if bugs arise.

In the end, choosing the correct architecture depends on several factors: team size, expected volume of access, need for flexibility in technologies, budget for infrastructure maintenance and urgency in time to market. Microservices and containers are not a silver bullet: they solve certain problems, but add others. Monolithic MVC frameworks bring initial simplicity, but can become difficult to maintain as the project grows or when multiple teams operate simultaneously. The 2025 ecosystem evolution offers many tools, but requires the team to carefully evaluate the implications of each decision.

In summary, modern web application architectures are characterized by the adoption of established standards (MVC, MVVM, etc.), integration between different services and scalability facilitated by the use of containers and orchestrators such as Docker and Kubernetes. Comparing different approaches shows that there is no single perfect solution: monoliths may be easy to get started, but microservices favor independence and scalability. At the same time, the choice between MVC or MVVM depends on the type of application – whether server-side or client-side – and the expected level of complexity. Containerization and orchestration tools enable applications to grow without severely impacting performance, but they require a robust CI/CD pipeline and observability practices, with centralized logs and metrics.

The movement towards distributed and event-based architectures reinforces the need for coherent design, which ensures the harmonious integration of all services and modules. Teams that adopt this model take advantage of independent releases, component-specific scalability, and rapid updates without impacting the entire application. However, the multiplicity of services requires careful governance: logs, security, API versioning and consistent data management become essential issues, resolved by good practices and market tools.

In the end, the choice of Flask or FastAPI as the basis for a microservice – or the decision to maintain parts of the system in an MVC monolith – is dictated by the needs of the domain, the pace of development, and the team's preferences. By 2025, the Python ecosystem offers solutions for all of these scenarios, from minimalist frameworks to highly complex cloud orchestration. True competitive advantage lies in the ability to choose the right architecture at the right time, balancing simplicity, scalability and long-term maintainability.

CHAPTER 24. FRONTEND INTEGRATION AND API CONSUMPTION

Integration between backend and frontend is one of the pillars of modern web applications. While the backend manages business rules, security and data persistence, the frontend is responsible for displaying and manipulating this information interactively. Communication between these two layers occurs through APIs, using standards such as REST and GraphQL. Technologies such as React, Vue.js and Angular are widely used to consume these APIs, allowing the creation of dynamic and efficient interfaces.

The separation between frontend and backend provides significant advantages, such as greater modularity and scalability. A backend developed in Flask or FastAPI can serve different clients, including web applications, mobile applications and even embedded systems. This approach facilitates system maintenance and evolution, as each layer can be developed and deployed independently.

A **CORS (Cross-Origin Resource Sharing) configuration** It is a fundamental aspect to ensure secure communication between different domains. Without this configuration, modern browsers block requests between different origins as a security measure. Frameworks like Flask and FastAPI natively support CORS through specialized libraries.

Below is an example of CORS configuration in a FastAPI backend:

python

```
# EXAMPLE 1: CORS configuration in FastAPI
from fastapi import FastAPI
from fastapi.middleware.cors import CORSMiddleware

app = FastAPI()

app.add_middleware(
    CORSMiddleware,
    allow_origins=["*"], # List of allowed origins
    allow_credentials=True,
    allow_methods=["GET", "POST", "PUT", "DELETE"],
    allow_headers=["*"],
)

@app.get("/data")
def get_data():
    return {"message": "API accessible by frontend"}
```

The parameter allow_origins defines which domains can access the API. In the production environment, it is recommended to restrict this list to avoid vulnerabilities.

In Flask, CORS configuration can be done with the extension Flask-CORS:

python

```
# EXAMPLE 2: CORS configuration in Flask
from flask import Flask, jsonify
from flask_cors import CORS

app = Flask(__name__)
CORS(app) # Enable CORS for all broken as

@app.route("/data")
def get_data():
    return jsonify({"message": "API accessible by frontend"})
```

Enabling CORS allows frontend applications to consume backend endpoints without restrictions imposed by the browser.

Consuming APIs with JavaScript Frameworks

On the frontend, the consumption of APIs can be done through different libraries and frameworks. Fetch API and Axios are the most common approaches for interacting with REST services.

Using the Fetch API to consume a FastAPI API:

javascript

```
// EXAMPLE 3: Consuming API with Fetch API
fetch("http://localhost:8000/data")
  .then(response => response.json())
  .then(data => console.log(data))
  .catch(error => console.error("Error fetching data:", error));
```

Using Axios to consume a Flask API:

javascript

```
// EXAMPLE 4: Consuming API with Axios
axios.get("http://localhost:5000/data")
  .then(response => console.log(response.data))
  .catch(error => console.error("Error fetching data:", error));
```

Axios makes it easy to handle responses, handle errors, and configure HTTP headers.

Authentication and Security in Communication

Secure integration between frontend and backend involves user authentication and data protection. Using JWT tokens (JSON Web Token) is a widely adopted practice for token-based authentication.

Generating and validating JWT in FastAPI:

python

```python
# EXAMPLE 5: Authentication with JWT in FastAPI
from fastapi import FastAPI, Depends, HTTPException
from fastapi.security import OAuth2PasswordBearer
import jwt

app = FastAPI()
oauth2_scheme = OAuth2PasswordBearer(tokenUrl="token")

SECRET_KEY = "supersecretkey"

def verify_token(token: str = Depends(oauth2_scheme)):
    try:
        payload = jwt.decode(token, SECRET_KEY,
algorithms=["HS256"])
        return payload
    except jwt.ExpiredSignatureError:
        raise HTTPException(status_code=401, detail="Token
expirado")
    except jwt.InvalidTokenError:
        raise HTTPException(status_code=401, detail="Token
inválido")

@app.get("/protected")
def protected_route(user_data: dict = Depends(verify_token)):
    return {"message": "Access authorized", "user": user_data}
```

This implementation protects routes, allowing access only to users authenticated with a valid token.

On the frontend, the JWT can be stored in the **localStorage** or **sessionStorage**, being sent in subsequent requests:

javascript

```javascript
// EXAMPLE 6: Sending JWT in Axios
const token = localStorage.getItem("token");

axios.get("http://localhost:8000/protected", {
  headers: { Authorization: `Bearer ${token}` }
})
  .then(response => console.log(response.data))
  .catch(error => console.error("Access denied:", error));
```

Using tokens eliminates the need for persistent server sessions, making authentication more scalable.

Practical Example of Integration

A real application might contain a form on the frontend for user authentication and a backend that validates credentials and returns a JWT token.

Frontend (React)
javascript

```javascript
// EXAMPLE 7: Login Form in React
import React, { useState } from "react";
import axios from "axios";

function Login() {
  const [email, setEmail] = useState("");
  const [password, setPassword] = useState("");

  const handleLogin = async () => {
    try {
      const response = await axios.post("http://localhost:8000/token", {
        email,
        password,
      });
      localStorage.setItem("token", response.data.token);
```

```
    alert("Login successful!");
  } catch (error) {
    alert("Error logging in");
  }
};

  return (
    <div>
      <h2>Login</h2>
      <input type="text" placeholder="E-mail" onChange={(e)
=> setEmail(e.target.value)} />
      <input type="password" placeholder="Senha"
onChange={(e) => setPassword(e.target.value)} />
      <button onClick={handleLogin}>Entrar</button>
    </div>
  );
}

export default Login;
```

Backend (FastAPI)
python

```python
# EXAMPLE 8: Authentication with JWT and FastAPI
from fastapi import FastAPI, HTTPException
import jwt
import datetime

app = FastAPI()

SECRET_KEY = "supersecretkey"

@app.post("/token")
def generate_token(email: str, password: str):
    if email == "admin@example.com" and password ==
"password":
        expiration = datetime.datetime.utcnow() +
```

```
datetime.timedelta(hours=1)
    token = jwt.encode({"sub": email, "exp": expiration},
SECRET_KEY, algorithm="HS256")
    return {"token": token}
  raise HTTPException(status_code=401, detail="Invalid
credentials")
```

This implementation allows a user to log in via the frontend, receive a JWT token, and use it to access protected routes.

Integration between frontend and backend is a central aspect of web development. REST and GraphQL APIs allow different platforms to consume the same services, ensuring reusability and scalability. The use of modern frameworks makes it easier to consume these APIs, while security practices such as CORS and JWT authentication ensure secure communication.

The advancement of web technologies requires developers to understand not only how to create APIs, but also the best ways to consume and protect them. Choosing the correct architecture, appropriate use of tokens and efficient integration between services are determining factors for building robust and secure applications.

CHAPTER 25. REAL USE CASES AND CASE STUDIES

The practical application of frameworks such as Flask and FastAPI in the development of web solutions has significantly impacted several industries. From startups to large corporations, companies are adopting these technologies to create scalable APIs, efficient microservices, and high-performance applications. Analyzing real projects allows you to understand how these tools are used to solve concrete problems, optimizing processes and driving innovation.

Successful Projects with Flask and FastAPI

Companies that adopted Flask and FastAPI saw significant gains in performance, scalability and development simplicity. Large platforms such as Netflix, Uber and Airbnb use Python in the backend, taking advantage of the language's flexibility for data manipulation, machine learning and communication between services.

Netflix: Microservices and APIs with Python

Netflix is one of the most notable examples of using Python for the backend. Although it has adopted several languages and frameworks, Python has become essential for automation, data analysis and microservices. Flask was used to create internal APIs and support content recommendation services.

One of the challenges Netflix faced was ensuring efficient communication between thousands of microservices. To achieve this, the company adopted **FastAPI** in some critical services, exploiting their ability to handle asynchronous calls and efficient data validation.

A simplified example of how a recommendation service can be implemented in **FastAPI**:

python

```python
# EXAMPLE 1: Recommendation API with FastAPI
from fastapi import FastAPI
import random

app = FastAPI()

recommendations = {
    "user_1": ["Stranger Things", "Breaking Bad", "The Witcher"],
    "user_2": ["Black Mirror", "Dark", "Narcos"],
}

@app.get("/recommend/{user_id}")
def get_recommendations(user_id: str):
    return {"recommendations":
recommendations.get(user_id, ["No recommendations
available"])}
```

This service can be easily integrated into the Netflix frontend or other internal systems. Choosing FastAPI guaranteed the company reduced response times, automatically validating JSON and using data typing efficiently.

Uber: Real-Time Data Processing

Uber faced challenges related to **Real-time processing of millions of requests**. The need to quickly respond to events such as driver calls and fare calculations led the company to adopt distributed architectures based on Python and messaging systems such as Kafka.

Flask was initially used to build internal driver management and route calculation APIs. As the platform grew, FastAPI began to be used in asynchronous services, allowing it to handle large volumes of requests without compromising latency.

An example of an API used to calculate fees can be seen below:

python

```python
# EXAMPLE 2: Rate Calculation API with FastAPI
from fastapi import FastAPI
from pydantic import BaseModel

app = FastAPI()

class RideRequest(BaseModel):
    distance_km: float
    time_minutes: float
    surge_multiplier: float

@app.post("/calculate_fare")
def calculate_fare(request: RideRequest):
    base_fare = 5.00
    cost_per_km = 2.50
    cost_per_minute = 0.50
    fare = (base_fare + (request.distance_km * cost_per_km)
+ (request.time_minutes * cost_per_minute)) *
request.surge_multiplier
    return {"fare": round(fare, 2)}
```

Integrating this service with mobile apps and dispatch systems has provided Uber with a highly scalable and responsive model.

Airbnb: Reservation Management with Flask

Airbnb needed an architecture that supported **high traffic loads**, ensuring that millions of users could search and book accommodation simultaneously. Flask was chosen for several internal services, especially for communication between search and payment systems.

An essential service on Airbnb is the availability of properties for booking. This system can be modeled with Flask as follows:

python

```
# EXAMPLE 3: Property Availability API with Flask
from flask import Flask, request, jsonify

app = Flask(__name__)

listings = {
    "101": {"city": "São Paulo", "available": True},
    "102": {"city": "Rio de Janeiro", "available": False},
}

@app.route("/availability/<listing_id>", methods=["GET"])
def check_availability(listing_id):
    listing = listings.get(listing_id, None)
    if listing:
        return jsonify({"available": listing["available"]})
    return jsonify({"error": "Property not found"}), 404
```

This endpoint allows search systems to quickly query property availability. Airbnb invested in optimizing REST APIs, using caching and distributed databases to ensure high performance.

Lessons Learned and Challenges Faced

Using Flask and FastAPI in large-scale systems has brought benefits and challenges. Some lessons learned from real projects include:

1. **Flask is great for smaller applications and lightweight APIs**, while FastAPI excels in asynchronous, high-performance systems.
2. **Data validation with Pydantic in FastAPI reduces errors and increases API reliability**.

3. **Scalability can be improved with containers and Kubernetes orchestration.**
4. **APIs must be well documented** to facilitate integration with other teams.

One of the biggest challenges was ensuring that **APIs continued to perform as traffic grew**. Strategies like **caching with Redis**, load balancing and database optimizations were essential to the success of the implementations.

Real Impact of Technologies on Industry

The evolution of web development with Flask and FastAPI has transformed several sectors. companies **fintech** utilize FastAPI to validate transactions in real-time, while streaming services rely on Flask to efficiently distribute content.

The industry of **e-commerce** benefited from creating scalable APIs to manage shopping carts and inventory in real time. An example of a cart management service can be implemented with FastAPI:

python

```python
# EXAMPLE 4: Shopping Cart API with FastAPI
from fastapi import FastAPI, HTTPException
from pydantic import BaseModel

app = FastAPI()

cart = {}

class CartItem(BaseModel):
    product_id: str
    quantity: int

@app.post("/add_to_cart")
def add_to_cart(item: CartItem):
    if item.product_id in cart:
        cart[item.product_id]["quantity"] += item.quantity
```

```
else:
    cart[item.product_id] = {"quantity": item.quantity}
return {"message": "Item added to cart", "cart": cart}
```

This type of API is widely used by retail platforms to offer personalized experiences to users.

Flask and FastAPI are fundamental tools in the development of modern web applications. Leading companies have adopted these technologies to build scalable and efficient services. The study of real cases shows that:

- **Flask is ideal for simple APIs and smaller applications**, while FastAPI stands out in **Asynchronous, high-performance APIs.**
- FastAPI's data validation and automatic documentation speeds development.
- The use of containers and microservices improves scalability.
- Integration with databases and caching techniques guarantee fast response.

The challenges faced in platform growth required performance optimizations, load balancing and enhanced security. The real impact of Flask and FastAPI on the industry continues to grow, driving innovation and enabling the creation of increasingly robust and efficient solutions.

CHAPTER 26. PERFORMANCE OPTIMIZATION IN WEB APPLICATIONS

The performance of a web application directly influences the user experience and system efficiency. Applications that load quickly and respond with low latency retain more users, reduce infrastructure costs and ensure scalability. Techniques such as code optimization, efficient database use, caching implementation and content distribution via CDN are essential strategies for achieving high performance.

Optimization starts from system architecture to code implementation. Applications developed with Flask and FastAPI can be enhanced using modern asynchronous processing, response compression, and database indexing techniques. Furthermore, continuous monitoring allows you to identify bottlenecks and take corrective actions.

Code Optimization Techniques and Queries

One of the main factors that affect the performance of a web application is code efficiency. Functions that process large volumes of data, poorly structured database queries and unnecessary locks can degrade performance.

Code Optimization in Flask and FastAPI

Code organization and efficient use of asynchronous processing can reduce API latency. In Flask, which operates synchronously, it is essential to avoid blocking operations on the main thread. In FastAPI, taking advantage of asynchronous support, operations involving database requests or external calls can be performed with async and await.

python

```
# EXAMPLE 1: Improving performance with async in FastAPI
from fastapi import FastAPI
import httpx

app = FastAPI()

async def fetch_data():
    async with httpx.AsyncClient() as client:
        response = await client.get("https://api.exemplo.com/data")
        return response.json()

@app.get("/data")
async def get_data():
    data = await fetch_data()
    return {"fetched_data": data}
```

The advantage of async is that other requests can be processed while the API waits for the response from the external server. This prevents the application from being blocked, allowing greater efficiency in the use of available resources.

Database Query Optimization

The database can be one of the main performance bottlenecks. Poorly structured queries can increase response time, consuming more server resources.

Proper indexing and **efficient use of queries** are fundamental.

sql

```
-- EXAMPLE 2: Creating an index to optimize searches
CREATE INDEX idx_users_email ON users(email);
```

Using ORMs like SQLAlchemy allows you to optimize queries by avoiding SELECT *, which brings unnecessary data.

python

```
# EXAMPLE 3: Queries optimized with SQLAlchemy
from sqlalchemy.orm import Session
from models import User

def get_user_by_email(db: Session, email: str):
    return db.query(User.id, User.name).filter(User.email ==
email).first()
```

By specifying only the required fields (id, name), the amount of data transferred is reduced, improving performance.

Caching Implementation and CDN Usage

Caching reduces the need for repetitive database queries by temporarily storing responses. Flask and FastAPI can use Redis to store frequently accessed data, improving response speed.

python

```
# EXAMPLE 4: Response caching with Redis on FastAPI
import redis
from fastapi import FastAPI

app = FastAPI()
cache = redis.Redis(host="localhost", port=6379,
decode_responses=True)

@app.get("/data/{item_id}")
def get_data(item_id: str):
    cached_data = cache.get(item_id)
    if cached_data:
        return {"cached": True, "data": cached_data}
```

```
data = f"Result processed for {item_id}"
cache.setex(item_id, 60, data) # Cache valid for 60 seconds
return {"cached": False, "data": data}
```

In addition to the internal cache, **Content Delivery Networks (CDNs)** how Cloudflare and Amazon CloudFront distribute static content globally, reducing loading latency.

nginx

```
# EXAMPLE 5: Configuring NGINX for CDN use
location /static/ {
    root /var/www/html;
    expires 30d;
    add_header Cache-Control "public, max-age=2592000";
}
```

This configuration allows browsers to store static files locally, reducing unnecessary requests.

Metrics Monitoring and Analysis

Tracking real-time metrics helps identify issues before they impact users. Tools like **Prometheus and Grafana** provide detailed monitoring, while structured logs make it easy to debug errors.

In FastAPI, you can integrate middleware to collect statistics on response time and error rate.

python

```
# EXAMPLE 6: Monitoring middleware in FastAPI
from fastapi import FastAPI, Request
import time

app = FastAPI()
```

```python
@app.middleware("http")
async def log_request_time(request: Request, call_next):
    start_time = time.time()
    response = await call_next(request)
    process_time = time.time() - start_time
    print(f"Request {request.url} demorou {process_time:.2f}
s")
    return response
```

This middleware records the execution time of each request, helping to identify slow endpoints.

Tools for Continuous Improvement

Performance optimization is an ongoing process. The use of **profilers**, **load test** and **fine adjustments** are fundamental to keeping the system efficient.

- **Locust**: tool to simulate multiple requests and measure the impact on the server.
- **New Relic**: analysis of response time and bottlenecks in the application.
- **Blackfire**: profiler to identify snippets of code that impact performance.

Locust can be used to simulate load and check the server response:

python

```python
# EXAMPLE 7: Load Testing with Locust
from locust import HttpUser, task

class WebsiteTest(HttpUser):
    @task
    def test_index(self):
        self.client.get("/")
```

Running locust -f test.py, it is possible to analyze how the API responds to thousands of simultaneous requests.

Performance optimization involves a variety of techniques that range from code organization to system infrastructure.

- Database queries must be optimized with efficient indexes and queries.
- Caching reduces the need to recompute frequently accessed data.
- Content distribution via CDN improves static file loading.
- Continuous monitoring allows you to identify problems before they impact the user experience.

The application of these strategies guarantees fast, scalable and reliable systems, ready to meet high demand without loss of efficiency.

CHAPTER 27. DEPENDENCY MANAGEMENT AND VIRTUAL ENVIRONMENTS

Building modern web applications requires efficient dependency management to ensure stability, security and reproducibility of the development environment. The use of virtual environments and tools such as pipenv and poetry allows you to keep packages organized, avoid conflicts between versions and ensure that applications run on any machine without unwanted dependencies.

Virtual environments create an isolated space where packages are installed separately from the operating system, allowing different projects to use different versions of libraries without interference. Modern tools also enable automatic resolution of dependencies, making code maintenance easier.

Creation and Maintenance of Isolated Environments

Python provides the module venv, which allows you to create virtual environments directly from the command line. To create a virtual environment in a project, use the following command:

bash

```
# Creating a virtual environment
python -m venv venv
```

This command generates a folder venv inside the project directory, containing an isolated copy of the Python interpreter. To activate the virtual environment:

Linux/macOS:
bash

source venv/bin/activate

Windows:
bash

venv\Scripts\activate

After activating the environment, any package installation will be done exclusively within it, without affecting the system.

To disable the virtual environment and return to the system global environment:

bash

deactivate

Use of pipenv for Dependency Management

THE pipenv is a modern alternative to venv, combining a virtual environment manager with an advanced package management system. It uses a file Pipfile to store project dependencies, ensuring consistency between installations on different machines.

Installing the pipenv can be done with pip:

bash

pip install pipenv

To create a virtual environment and install dependencies:

bash

```
pipenv install
```

To add specific packages to the project:

bash

```
pipenv install requests
```

THE pipenv stores package versions in Pipfile.lock, ensuring that all future installations use exactly the same versions, avoiding inconsistencies between development and production environments.

Dependency Management with poetry

THE poetry is another advanced tool that simplifies package and version management. It allows you to install and update libraries efficiently using a file pyproject.toml to register project settings.

To install the poetry:

bash

```
pip install poetry
```

To start a new project and configure its dependencies:

bash

```
poetry init
poetry add fastapi
```

One of the advantages of poetry is the ability to automatically lock package versions, avoiding conflicts and ensuring that different developers use exactly the same versions.

Version Control and Package Updates

Keeping dependencies updated is essential to ensure security and compatibility with new framework versions. THE pip allows you to check which packages are out of date:

bash

```
pip list --outdated
```

To update a specific package:

bash

```
pip install --upgrade package_name
```

No pipenv, the package update is done with:

bash

```
pipenv update package_name
```

Already in poetry, the equivalent command is:

bash

```
poetry update package_name
```

The use of **requirements files** (requirements.txt) also makes it easy to quickly install all of a project's dependencies. To generate a requirements file:

bash

```
pip freeze > requirements.txt
```

To install all dependencies listed in the file:

bash

```
pip install -r requirements.txt
```

Strategies to Avoid Conflicts and Bugs

Conflicting dependencies can cause unexpected application failures. Some good practices help minimize these problems:

- **Always use virtual environments** to avoid interference between projects.
- **Specify package versions** no requirements.txt, Pipfile or pyproject.toml to ensure reproducibility.
- **Test package updates** before applying them in production, avoiding incompatibilities.
- **Use audit tools** as pip-audit to check packages for known vulnerabilities.

bash

```
pip install pip-audit
pip-audit
```

This approach helps identify outdated libraries or libraries with security holes, ensuring a reliable development environment.

Efficient management of dependencies and virtual environments is a fundamental pillar for developing robust and scalable applications. Tools like venv, pipenv and poetry offer secure and organized methods for installing and updating packages, avoiding conflicts and ensuring that applications run consistently across different environments.

The use of these practices allows for greater code stability, facilitating collaboration between developers and the maintenance of long-term projects. Implementing strict controls over dependencies reduces unexpected failures and improves application security.

CHAPTER 28. COMPLEMENTARY TOOLS AND LIBRARIES

Efficiency in developing web applications with Flask and FastAPI can be improved by using complementary libraries and tools. The Python ecosystem offers a variety of packages to handle HTTP communication, asynchronous task queues, monitoring, profiling, and integration with external services. Knowing and using these resources allows you to develop more robust, scalable and efficient applications.

Useful Libraries for Development

Python has a vast set of libraries that facilitate the implementation of various functionalities in APIs and web applications. Some of the most used include:

- **requests**: sending HTTP requests in a simple and efficient way.
- **httpx**: asynchronous alternative to requests, ideal for FastAPI.
- **celery**: asynchronous processing and task queue management.
- **apscheduler**: scheduling recurring tasks.
- **log**: Advanced log management.
- **pydantic**: data validation and structuring in FastAPI.

Each of these libraries plays a key role in improving productivity and creating optimized applications.

Use of requests for HTTP Requests

THE requests It is widely used for consuming APIs and integrating with external services.

python

```python
# EXAMPLE 1: API consumption with requests
import requests

response = requests.get("https://api.example.com/data")

if response.status_code == 200:
    data = response.json()
    print(data)
else:
    print("Error fetching data")
```

For asynchronous applications, the httpx is a more efficient alternative.

python

```python
# EXAMPLE 2: Asynchronous request with httpx
import httpx
import asyncio

async def fetch_data():
    async with httpx.AsyncClient() as client:
        response = await client.get("https://api.exemplo.com/
data")
        return response.json()

asyncio.run(fetch_data())
```

Asynchronous processing with celery

THE celery is a popular solution for asynchronous task processing, allowing time-consuming operations to run in the background without blocking the application.

python

```python
# EXAMPLE 3: Basic Celery Configuration
```

```
from celery import Celery

app = Celery("tasks", broker="redis://localhost:6379/0")

@app.task
def add(x, y):
    return x + y
```

This structure allows tasks to be queued and processed efficiently, ensuring scalability.

Task Scheduling with apscheduler

THE apscheduler enables the execution of automatic tasks at pre-defined times, such as backups and notifications.

python

```
#EXAMPLE 4: Scheduling recurring tasks
from apscheduler.schedulers.background import
BackgroundScheduler
import time

def task():
    print("Task executed")

scheduler = BackgroundScheduler()
scheduler.add_job(tarefa, "interval", seconds=10)
scheduler.start()

try:
    while True:
        time.sleep(2)
except (KeyboardInterrupt, SystemExit):
    scheduler.shutdown()
```

This mechanism is useful for processes that must be run periodically without manual intervention.

Integration with External Services and Third-Party APIs

External APIs are widely used to integrate with services such as payments, notifications and data analysis.

Integration with Stripe API

Payment platforms like Stripe offer REST APIs to process transactions securely.

python

```
# EXAMPLE 5: Integration with Stripe API
import stripe

stripe.api_key = "your_secret_key"

payment_intent = stripe.PaymentIntent.create(
    amount=5000,
    currency="usd",
    payment_method_types=["card"],
)

print(payment_intent)
```

This integration allows payments to be processed without the need for a complex banking system.

Debugging and Profiling Tools

Code profiling helps you identify performance bottlenecks and optimize the execution of APIs.

Use of log for Log Monitoring

THE log is a library that improves the log system, offering a simplified syntax and better structuring of messages.

python

```
# EXAMPLE 6: Configuring logs with Loguru
```

```
from loguru import logger

logger.add("app.log", format="{time} {level} {message}",
level="INFO")

logger.info("Application started")
logger.error("Critical error detected")
```

Logs are essential for diagnosing failures and monitoring application behavior.

Code Profiling with cProfile

THE cProfile It can be used to measure the execution time of functions, identifying points that need optimization.

python

```
# EXAMPLE 7: Code profiling with cProfile
import cProfile

def process_data():
    result = sum(range(1000000))
    return result

cProfile.run("process_data()")
```

This approach allows for strategic adjustments to improve code efficiency.

Practical Examples of Complementary Application

Complementary libraries and tools can be combined to create robust solutions.

Example: Asynchronous API with Background Processing

This API uses FastAPI, Celery, and Redis to process background tasks.

python

```
# EXAMPLE 8: FastAPI with Celery for asynchronous
processing
from fastapi import FastAPI
from celery import Celery

app = FastAPI()
celery_app = Celery("tasks", broker="redis://
localhost:6379/0")

@celery_app.task
def process_data(data):
    return {"processed_data": data.upper()}

@app.post("/submit_task/")
def submit_task(data: str):
    task = process_data.delay(data)
    return {"task_id": task.id}
```

With this implementation, the API accepts requests and processes data without blocking system execution.

The use of complementary tools and libraries in web development with Flask and FastAPI expands the possibilities and facilitates the creation of more performant, scalable and secure applications.

Efficient integration with external APIs, asynchronous processing and implementation of structured logs optimize maintenance and ensure a better experience for users and developers. With the right choice of libraries, it is possible to reduce development time and increase the reliability of applications.

CHAPTER 29. TRENDS AND INNOVATIONS IN WEB DEVELOPMENT WITH PYTHON

Web development is constantly evolving, driven by the emergence of new technologies, frameworks and architectural patterns. Python, being one of the most versatile and widely adopted languages, continues to play a fundamental role in this scenario, especially with the advancement of artificial intelligence, automation and microservices. Frameworks like FastAPI and Flask are increasingly popular due to their flexibility, support for modern APIs, and efficiency in asynchronous processing.

Innovations in the sector include the use of artificial intelligence in application optimization, the growth of serverless development, the adoption of microservices-based architectures and the use of low-code/no-code technologies to accelerate development. Additionally, evolving DevOps practices and the continuous integration of observability tools are shaping the future of web applications.

New Technologies and Emerging Frameworks

Development frameworks are increasingly focused on performance, scalability and compatibility with modern web standards. Some of the most impactful trends include:

- **FastAPI as the standard for high-performance APIs**: Due to its native support for asynchronous operations and automatic data validation.
- **Django 4+ and the evolution of its features**: remains one

of the leading frameworks for full-stack development, now with improved support for WebSockets and asynchronous components.

- **BentoML and the integration of machine learning in web applications**: A framework that enables rapid deployment of machine learning models for APIs and web services.
- **Refinement of serverless frameworks like Zappa**: facilitating the deployment of Python applications directly to services such as AWS Lambda.

Serverless architecture and microservices have stood out as efficient approaches for scalability and maintenance of distributed applications.

Example: Using FastAPI for Asynchronous Microservices

Asynchronous programming and the ability to process multiple requests simultaneously made FastAPI the ideal choice for microservices-based applications.

python

```python
# EXAMPLE 1: Asynchronous service in FastAPI for user query
from fastapi import FastAPI
import httpx

app = FastAPI()

async def fetch_user(user_id: int):
    async with httpx.AsyncClient() as client:
        response = await client.get(f"https://api.example.com/users/{user_id}")
        return response.json()

@app.get("/user/{user_id}")
async def get_user(user_id: int):
    user_data = await fetch_user(user_id)
    return {"user": user_data}
```

This model allows the API to execute external calls without blocking other requests, ensuring greater efficiency.

Impact of Artificial Intelligence and Machine Learning

Artificial intelligence is redefining the way web applications work, enabling process automation, real-time data analysis and dynamic content personalization.

Among the most notable advances is the integration of **machine learning models** directly in APIs, allowing the creation of more intelligent systems.

Example: Machine Learning API with FastAPI and scikit-learn

Using FastAPI combined with libraries like scikit-learn allows you to expose predictive models directly as endpoints of a web application.

python

```python
# EXAMPLE 2: Machine Learning API for price prediction
from fastapi import FastAPI
import pickle
import numpy as np

app = FastAPI()

# Loading previously trained model
with open("modelo_precos.pkl", "rb") as file:
    modelo = pickle.load(file)

@app.get("/predict/")
def predict(value: float, size: float):
    data = np.array([[value, size]])
    prediction = model.predict(data)
    return {"estimated_price": prediction[0]}
```

This API can be integrated with dynamic pricing systems,

optimizing the user experience with real-time responses.

Evolution of Development Practices

Web development has become more modular and agile, with new practices being incorporated to ensure greater efficiency and security. Some trends include:

- **Event-based architecture**: Use of queues and asynchronous messages to decouple components and improve scalability.
- **Infrastructure as Code (IaC)**: use of tools such as Terraform and Ansible to manage servers and cloud services in an automated way.
- **Continuous integration and continuous delivery (CI/CD)**: tools like GitHub Actions and GitLab CI/CD facilitate the automation of tests and deployments.

The event-based approach is particularly useful for distributed applications.

Example: Asynchronous Communication between Microservices with Kafka

Using messaging with Apache Kafka allows microservices to communicate efficiently without directly depending on each other.

python

```python
# EXAMPLE 3: Posting messages to a Kafka topic
from kafka import KafkaProducer
import json

producer = KafkaProducer(
    bootstrap_servers="localhost:9092",
    value_serializer=lambda v: json.dumps(v).encode("utf-8"),
)

message = {"event": "new_order", "order_id": 12345}
```

```
producer.send("orders", message)
```

This model reduces direct dependence between services, improving application resilience.

Future Perspectives and Opportunities

The future of web development with Python will be shaped by emerging technologies, including:

- **Growing use of WebAssembly (Wasm)**: allowing Python to run directly in the browser.
- **Advanced automation with artificial intelligence**: more sophisticated bots, chatbots and virtual assistants.
- **Expansion of serverless architectures**: lighter and more scalable applications.
- **Adoption of new security and privacy standards**: improvement in the processing of sensitive data.

The evolution of tools and the advancement of cloud-based infrastructure will continue to allow applications to be developed and scaled efficiently.

Web development with Python will continue to evolve with the introduction of new technologies, frameworks, and architectural patterns. Artificial intelligence, microservices, asynchronous programming and serverless architectures are trends that will shape the future of applications, providing greater efficiency, scalability and security.

Mastering these technologies opens up significant opportunities for developers and companies, allowing the construction of innovative solutions prepared for the challenges of the future.

CHAPTER 30. STRATEGIES FOR MAINTENANCE AND EVOLUTION OF WEB PROJECTS

Maintaining and evolving a web project requires planning, organization and application of good development practices. An application's longevity depends on its ability to adapt to new technologies, ongoing code maintenance, and clear documentation to ensure that different developers can understand and improve the system over time.

The success of a web project lies not only in its launch, but in the way it remains efficient and relevant over the years. Refactoring, updating dependencies, code optimization and constant monitoring are fundamental strategies to ensure that the application continues to operate in a stable and secure manner.

Long-Term Planning and Project Management

Software development must be treated as a continuous cycle, where each phase includes improvements, corrections and optimizations. The application of agile methodologies and DevOps practices facilitates the maintenance and evolution of systems.

An effective approach to keeping projects organized is to divide tasks into short cycles, such as sprints, allowing for incremental deliveries.

Example: Organizing Tasks with GitHub Projects

Using project management tools helps you track task progress and optimize the development flow.

yaml

```
#EXAMPLE 1: GitHub Projects configuration file
name: Continuous Development
columns:
  - name: Backlog
  - name: In Progress
  - name: Review
  - name: Completed
```

This model organizes demands and allows you to visualize the stage of each task within the development cycle.

Techniques for Refactoring and Continuous Update

Refactoring is essential to maintain code quality and improve code efficiency. Legacy code can become a problem if not reviewed periodically.

Updating libraries and frameworks is also essential to ensure security and compatibility with new versions.

Example: Identification of Obsolete Code

The use of tools such as pylint and flake8 helps identify code patterns that need to be fixed.

bash

```
pip install pylint flake8
pylint my_project/
flake8 my_project/
```

These tools analyze the code and point out sections that need to be refactored to improve readability and efficiency.

Refactoring with Code Standards

Organizing the code and removing unnecessary repetition makes the system more modular and easier to maintain.

python

```python
# EXAMPLE 2: Improving readability and code reuse
def process_user_data(user_id, action):
    user = get_user_from_db(user_id)
    if action == "activate":
        user.activate()
    elif action == "deactivate":
        user.deactivate()
    user.save()
```

This model reduces redundant code and facilitates future modifications.

Documentation, Training and Knowledge Transfer

Documentation is one of the most overlooked aspects, but also one of the most important. Projects without clear documentation become difficult to maintain and expand.

Using automated documentation tools makes it easier to share information among team members.

Generating Documentation with FastAPI

FastAPI natively supports automatic generation of interactive documentation.

python

```python
# EXAMPLE 3: Automatic documentation generation with
FastAPI
from fastapi import FastAPI

app = FastAPI(title="My API", description="Auto-generated
documentation")

@app.get("/items/{item_id}")
def read_item(item_id: int):
    return {"item_id": item_id}
```

Interactive documentation can be accessed through the Swagger UI, making the API easier to understand.

Using README and Wikis for Project Maintenance

Create a file README.md detailed helps new developers understand the project structure.

markdown

```
# My Project
This is a project developed with FastAPI for user management.
## Requirements
- Python 3.10+
- FastAPI
- Uvicorn
## Installation
```bash
pip install -r requirements.txt
uvicorn main:app --reload
```

pgsql

This format ensures that anyone accessing the repository can quickly understand and use the code.

Scalability Planning and Adaptation to Change

The scalability of a project depends on the ability to adapt to new challenges and the efficient use of computational resources.

Adoption of containers, architecture based on microservices and the use of asynchronous queues are strategies that guarantee better performance.

Using Docker for Scalability
```

Docker allows you to package applications and their dependencies in a standardized way, facilitating scalability.

```dockerfile
# EXAMPLE 4: Dockerfile for FastAPI application
FROM python:3.10
WORKDIR /app
COPY requirements.txt .
RUN pip install --no-cache-dir -r requirements.txt
COPY . .
CMD ["uvicorn", "main:app", "--host", "0.0.0.0", "--port", "8000"]
```

This model ensures that the application runs consistently across different environments.

Monitoring with Prometheus and Grafana

Maintaining a scalable system involves collecting and analyzing metrics to anticipate problems.

yaml

```yaml
# EXAMPLE 5: Basic Prometheus configuration for monitoring
global:
  scrape_interval: 15s

scrape_configs:
  - job_name: "fastapi_app"
    static_configs:
      - targets: ["localhost:8000"]
```

This approach allows you to view performance metrics in real time, ensuring better decision making.

The maintenance and evolution of web projects requires continuous planning, adoption of good development practices and tools that guarantee efficiency and security.

The implementation of refactoring, deployment automation, documentation and monitoring strategies facilitates long-term application management, ensuring that they remain stable, secure and scalable. With the right approach, any project can be maintained and improved efficiently without compromising its performance or security.

FINAL CONCLUSION

Web development in Python has experienced remarkable evolution over the years and, in 2025, it has become one of the main choices for creating APIs, microservices and high-performance applications. The wide variety of tools and frameworks available brings flexibility and agility to teams of all sizes, opening up space for innovation and modern approaches. The proposed journey covered each essential point to implement robust, secure and scalable projects, covering everything from basic HTTP concepts to advanced automation and microservices practices.

A **reflection on the evolution of web development with Python** reveals that the language has consolidated its space in several industries, supporting corporate applications, streaming platforms, financial services and e-commerce systems. The Python community has been active in producing libraries and frameworks that speed up the process of creating APIs and dynamic websites. The emergence of event-based architectures, the popularization of containers, and the use of automation and DevOps tools have expanded the scope even further. In this scenario, Flask and FastAPI stand out as powerful alternatives for backend development, whether in small applications or large-scale distributed systems.

The course of this work was divided into thirty chapters, each covering fundamental or specialized aspects of web development in Python. Below is a fluid recap:

Chapter 1. Introduction to Web Development with Python presented the historical context and evolution of web development, highlighting the role of Python in digital transformation. The chapter explored the overview of frameworks such as Flask and FastAPI, in addition to outlining the objectives and structure of the book, preparing the ground for the following steps.

Chapter 2. Configuring the Development Environment covered installing Python, using package managers, and configuring virtual environments. The choice of IDEs and editors, as well as initial setup practices, make every developer's work more efficient. The chapter reinforced the importance of organizing the environment to avoid version conflicts and speed up development.

Chapter 3. Python for Web Fundamentals served as a review of the basic concepts of the language, including control structures, data manipulation and module organization. The importance of following coding standards and maintaining readability ensures that code remains clear, even in large teams and projects that span many years.

Chapter 4. HTTP Concepts and RESTful APIs examined the HTTP protocol, methods such as GET and POST, status codes, and REST principles. Comparison with other API architectures clarified why REST is so popular and offered insights into how to design clean, consistent interfaces for internal or external consumption.

Chapter 5. Introduction to Flask presented the history and philosophy of the microframework, showing its advantages in terms of simplicity and flexibility. Installation, getting started, and the basic structure of a Flask application demonstrated how to quickly build APIs and routes, as well as emphasizing the importance of keeping the application organized.

Chapter 6. Structure and Routing in Flask explored details of configuration and route definition, as well as showing how to use decorators to map endpoints. It also discussed dynamic parameters and modular organization, essential for projects that grow over time. Good routing architecture facilitates maintenance and evolution of features.

Chapter 7. Templates and Rendering with Jinja2 explained the fundamentals of the Jinja2 template engine, the creation and organization of HTML templates, and inheritance and inclusion techniques. The ability to produce dynamic pages and manage complex layouts with template inheritance made the workflow more efficient. This chapter included practical examples of rendering and keeping code clean.

Chapter 8. Working with Forms and Validation covered the creation, processing and validation of forms, showing extensions such as Flask-WTF. The display of error messages and best data capture practices increase security and prevent quality problems when dealing with information sent by users.

Chapter 9. Integration with Databases in Flask described how to use SQLAlchemy and its ORM to configure connections, model data, and perform CRUD operations. It also dealt with migrations and versioning of schemes, reinforcing the importance of maintaining control of structural changes in the bank over time, ensuring consistency between development and production.

Chapter 10. Authentication and Authorization in Flask presented login methods, session management and use of extensions for security, such as Flask-Login. Access control and permissions were discussed, as well as strategies to protect sensitive data. This chapter highlighted the need to implement solid layers of security for applications that handle user information.

Chapter 11. Common Flask Errors and Troubleshooting brought problem diagnosis, debugging and log recording techniques. Tips for optimizing performance included tips on how to identify conflicts and resolve dependency errors that may arise. This chapter emphasized logging practices and tools that assist developers in test and production environments.

Chapter 12. Introduction to FastAPI began the transition to a more modern framework, focusing on asynchronous. The philosophy and differences of FastAPI were clear, as was the installation and initial configuration. There was a comparison with Flask, showing advantages and typical applications for each approach. The basic structure of a FastAPI application demonstrated how to create routes and endpoints in a simple and intuitive way.

Chapter 13. Creating APIs with FastAPI covered in detail the definition and creation of endpoints, the flow of requests and responses, as well as route parameters and query strings. Practical API examples were presented, always following the asynchronous model of the framework and highlighting the productivity and efficiency it provides.

Chapter 14. Typing and Validation with Pydantic focused on Pydantic capabilities for creating data models and automatic validation in FastAPI. The benefit of static typing brought greater reliability, avoiding typing errors and data inconsistency. Practical application cases in real scenarios were also shown, reinforcing how typing can improve the quality of development.

Chapter 15. Automatic Documentation with FastAPI explained how to generate interactive documentation with Swagger and Redoc. Route customization and the importance of documentation for the developer community were highlighted. Examples of good practices in the use and extension of these resources were discussed, making the APIs easy to consume by internal and external teams.

Chapter 16. Integration with Databases in FastAPI showed how to configure and use ORM with SQLAlchemy in a FastAPI environment, facilitating CRUD operations and maintaining model migrations and synchronization. Examples of queries and data manipulations were presented, as well as migration strategies to keep the schema updated.

Chapter 17. Authentication and Security in FastAPI discussed implementing robust authentication and authorization systems, as well as managing JWT and OAuth2 tokens. Strategies for access control, API security and the use of permissions and security policies were shown. This chapter emphasized the need to protect sensitive data and ensure that endpoints are only accessed by authorized users.

Chapter 18. Deploy and Scalability of Applications with FastAPI described the preparation of applications for production, the use of ASGI servers (uvicorn and hypercorn), as well as deployment strategies in containers and the cloud. The need for monitoring and scalability was clear, with mentions of container orchestrators and CI/CD best practices. This chapter reinforced the importance of an automation pipeline to handle updates and traffic growth.

Chapter 19. Testing and Code Quality for Web APIs explored the relevance of automated testing, setting up test environments (pytest, etc.), the search for high code coverage and analysis tools for continuous integration. Code quality directly reflects the project's ability to evolve, as test routines ensure that new features do not generate regressions.

Chapter 20. Good Practices and Code Standards it dealt with the adoption of standards such as PEP 8, refactoring and systematic code maintenance. Continuous integration and deployment (CI/CD), as well as the use of static analysis tools, keep the team informed about style issues, complexity and possible vulnerabilities. Standardization is essential for the work to remain consistent, regardless of how many developers work on the project.

Chapter 21. Debugging and Monitoring in Web Applications covered advanced debugging techniques, performance monitoring and logs, as well as the use of APM and incident response strategies. Continuous monitoring of metrics and detailed log analysis reduces the time to detect and fix problems, increasing application reliability.

Chapter 22. Microservices with Flask and FastAPI delved into the concepts and advantages of this distributed architecture, showing communication between services, the implementation of independent services and practical cases. The challenges of orchestration and observability in microservices were also discussed, highlighting the importance of a coherent design and distributed tracing tools to understand the journey of requests.

Chapter 23. Modern Web Application Architectures presented patterns such as MVC, MVVM and microservices, discussing the use of containers and orchestration with Docker and Kubernetes. The comparison between different approaches, whether a traditional monolith or distributed services, emphasized the careful choice based on the requirements of each project and the team profile.

Chapter 24. Frontend Integration and API Consumption talked about communication between backend and frontend, showing concepts of CORS, consumption of APIs in JavaScript frameworks and security in the exchange of information. The possibility of decoupled and scalable front-ends, combined with robust backends, expands the reach of solutions and facilitates the collaboration of teams specialized in each area.

Chapter 25. Real Use Cases and Case Studies showcased examples of success with Flask and FastAPI, exploring challenges faced and solutions adopted to deal with high demand and business complexity. The real impact of these technologies on the industry reinforced the relevance of Python in web development, showing that scalable projects can be built with these tools.

Chapter 26. Performance Optimization in Web Applications covered advanced code and query optimization techniques, caching implementation, and use of CDNs. Metric monitoring and analysis, in addition to continuous improvement tools, ensure that applications maintain good performance even under traffic spikes. This practice is essential for competitive environments where every millisecond can make a difference in the user experience.

Chapter 27. Dependency Management and Virtual Environments covered tools such as pipenv and poetry, highlighting the importance of maintaining isolated environments free from version conflicts. Continuously maintaining updated packages and adopting good versioning practices are crucial to avoiding bugs and preserving project reliability over time.

Chapter 28. Complementary Tools and Libraries showed useful packages, such as requests, celery, and debugging and profiling techniques. Integration with external services and third-party APIs becomes simpler when the developer knows the appropriate libraries to handle HTTP requests, asynchronous queues and performance monitoring. This set of tools makes it possible to create more complete and efficient solutions.

Chapter 29. Trends and Innovations in Web Development with Python discussed emerging technologies, the impact of artificial intelligence and machine learning, and the continuous evolution of development practices. In 2025, Python will remain relevant precisely because it follows these changes and offers support on several fronts, such as microservices, serverless and automation.

Chapter 30. Strategies for Maintenance and Evolution of Web Projects concluded with reflections on long-term planning, refactoring, documentation, training and scalability. Preparing to deal with technological and market changes ensures that the project remains viable and productive, without compromising its code base or its ability to grow.

Throughout these chapters, themes emerged such as creating simple Flask applications and using FastAPI to build high-performance APIs, organizing routes, structuring forms and validating data, using relational databases and applying migrations, protecting routes with login and JWT tokens, migrating to deployment in containers and scalability via Kubernetes, as well as integration with sophisticated front-ends and the adoption of good performance practices. Each topic complements the previous one, forming a solid framework for anyone who wants to completely master web development in Python.

This scope shows that it is not enough to know the basics of Python or a framework. The success of an application demands understanding protocols, data modeling, security, automated tests, logs and monitoring, caching and scalability strategies. In a world where technologies evolve rapidly, the ability to adapt and learn new concepts is essential. The use of containers, for example, has become practically standard in modern teams, as has the adoption of CI/CD to ensure frequent and reliable deliveries.

With each chapter, the reader was able to delve deeper into crucial areas of web development, learning about tools and libraries that simplify everyday tasks. Python's big difference is the combination of its friendly learning curve and the variety of resources available, which range from building microservices to integrating machine learning. The future indicates the consolidation of distributed architectures, the incorporation of AI to optimize processes and the even greater automation of deployment and monitoring routines.

The direction for future studies and practices includes the application of acquired knowledge. Projects that require high performance can benefit from the intensive use of coroutines, caching and good RESTful or GraphQL route design. On the other hand, solutions focused on data manipulation or reporting can take advantage of data science libraries, integrating them with Flask or FastAPI to generate analytical APIs. With the profusion of cloud providers, developers have serverless environments, managed containers and robust orchestration at their disposal. Testing and monitoring remain a priority, ensuring that innovations do not break functionality.

The creation of secure and scalable applications, based on the fundamentals explored, leads to varied opportunities in the market. Whether in fintechs that need ultra-secure routes, e-commerce platforms that demand high availability or startups that value the speed of delivery of MVPs, Python and its web development frameworks offer the ideal foundation. With the adoption of CI/CD pipelines, centralized logs, distributed tracing and autoscaling, the team now has greater confidence in the robustness of the system.

This content consolidates the main techniques, tools and concepts for building, maintaining and evolving web projects in Python. We hope that each reader, whether beginner or experienced professional, will find here a practical and inspiring guide to continue improving their skills, innovating and creating impactful solutions. The web development journey is dynamic and full of challenges, but also opportunities to transform ideas into products and services that benefit people and organizations.

Cordially,
Diego Rodrigues & Team!

www.ingramcontent.com/pod-product-compliance
Lightning Source LLC
LaVergne TN
LVHW051222050326
832903LV00028B/2209

*9 7 9 8 3 1 3 0 8 2 9 7 4 *